Happy Class

Happy Class

The Practical Guide
to Classroom Management

Jenna Sage

ROWMAN & LITTLEFIELD
Lanham • Boulder • New York • London

Published by Rowman & Littlefield
A wholly owned subsidiary of The Rowman & Littlefield Publishing Group, Inc.
4501 Forbes Boulevard, Suite 200, Lanham, Maryland 20706
www.rowman.com

Unit A, Whitacre Mews, 26-34 Stannary Street, London SE11 4AB

British Library Cataloguing in Publication Information Available

Library of Congress Cataloging-in-Publication Data

Names: Sage, Jenna, 1977-
Title: Happy class : the practical guide to classroom management / Jenna Sage.
Description: Lanham, Maryland : Rowman & Littlefield, 2017. | Includes index.
Identifiers: LCCN 2016042562 (print) | LCCN 2016043103 (ebook) | ISBN
  9781475824810 (cloth : alk. paper) | ISBN 9781475824841 (pbk. : alk.
  paper) | ISBN 9781475824858 (electronic)
Subjects: LCSH: Classroom management.
Classification: LCC LB3013 .S238 2017 (print) | LCC LB3013 (ebook) | DDC
  371.102/4—dc23
LC record available at https://lccn.loc.gov/2016042562

∞™ The paper used in this publication meets the minimum requirements of
American National Standard for Information Sciences—Permanence of Paper
for Printed Library Materials, ANSI/NISO Z39.48-1992.

Printed in the United States of America

Contents

Preface

I pulled up in front of the large, antiquated, brick school building. I truly had no conception of what the day might hold. I only knew that I was hired for the day to be a substitute classroom aide. I pushed the heavy glass-and-steel doors aside and found myself in the front office.

I had been a struggling student growing up. I was terrible at math. My brain just didn't seem to be wired for numbers. In the first grade, I began playing sick when math class began. I took a weekly, sometimes daily, trip to the nurse's office. Each time I missed math class, I fell deeper into the math gap.

As years passed, I tried to focus on my strengths. I loved writing, dancing, singing, acting, drama, and debate. As those same years passed, fewer and fewer opportunities to take creative courses availed themselves. School became hyperfocused on core content areas. I became hyperfocused on my inabilities rather than my abilities.

In high school I took every elective I could. However, electives didn't earn you the right credits to graduate. School lost its luster. Learning lost its shine. I fell back into old habits and began skipping classes. I skipped so many classes in tenth grade that I was told that graduation would be unlikely and I should not return.

I am the daughter of a teacher, a proud teacher. I am the product of a system that didn't focus on my skills, talents, abilities, and strengths. I am still a person who struggles to see my intelligence as a cup more than half-full rather than totally emptied.

As I stood in the office of the elementary school for my first day of work, I felt the electric buzz in the office, the students coming and going, the parents dropping off their children, and a teacher running copies and sipping coffee in a hurried pace. I felt energized. The place ran like a well-oiled machine.

I was assigned to a student in a kindergarten class. I could handle kindergarten; it was probably the last grade in which I felt truly comfortable. The day would likely be filled with tracing letters onto lined papers, playing house and blocks, and going out on the playground.

The student I was assigned to had severe ADHD. As I entered the classroom, he stood out from his peers. He was sitting on top of the desk singing loudly as the teacher attempted to share where the big and little hands were on the clock. The student grew bored of his own voice and began playing with items in a storage closet. The teacher grew more and more frustrated.

I received my orders during the first break in activity:

- "Keep him occupied."
- "Be sure to pay attention to him every second of the day."
- "Follow along with the class and try to get him to do some of the work."

Easy enough, I thought.

Within two hours, the student had made his way into a crevasse in the wall, and I couldn't find him. So much for learning letters; so much for me having a job the next day.

Early the next morning, my phone rang. It was the principal of the school. "We would like you to come back today and work with the same student, if you are willing." I was confused. "I don't understand. I didn't think I did a good job of watching him yesterday." The principal explained that the teacher had let her know at the end of the day that the student sat on his carpet square for thirty seconds during calendar time, which was the longest he had ever sat.

I worked one-on-one with that student for three years until he was fully integrated into a general education classroom without support. During those three years, I became a student again. Every day I learned more about the skill and art of teaching, the process of learning, the science of behavior, the patience of educators, the growth of children, and the importance of individuality.

I had bad days—terrible days—days in which I was hit, bitten, kicked, yelled at, and cursed at. I had amazing days—days where I saw the student grow, a "light bulb" click on, the family give hugs, the other students accept and welcome, and the other teachers express kindness and gratitude. I had days when I knew I couldn't ever be a teacher and days when I knew that was the only calling in my life.

After I was pushed out of high school, rather than remaining a high-school dropout, I graduated from an alternative school that focused on student strengths and helped students graduate by working toward feasible and meaningful credit-earning opportunities. It was not a traditional school, and it was full of kids who made bad choices, some terrible choices. But it was a school that had staff who cared about each and every one of us. They spent time getting to know us and focused on our talents. It was a community whose members would stop at nothing to help us so we would not become the forgotten ones.

This book is a culmination of my experiences, my learning, my growth, and my passion for ensuring that there are no forgotten ones. Each chapter and example are derived from personal experience and from all of my opportunities to learn from amazing educators.

For as much as I struggled in school, I want to thank those teachers who may not have believed in me. I want to thank those teachers who didn't notice me asking for or simply needing more help. Those teachers help to remind me how important positivity and happiness are. My experiences helped me to be a better person and a better educator.

I especially want to thank the teacher leaders in my life—my mom, first of all. I grew up vicariously in her classroom. I grew up in the shadow of her reputation. She was an amazing teacher whose impact on the children's lives is immeasurable. She encouraged me to take that substitute classroom aide position, and she has encouraged me every step of the way since then. From the day I was kicked out of high school through my graduation from the alternative school, receiving my bachelor's in psychology and my master's degree in special education, to receiving my doctorate in special education, she believed in me when I didn't. Her love of teaching and learning is woven deeply in every word of this book.

To my mentors: I so closely observed you and took diligent notes. I listened to advice. I spent years gaining from your experiences. When you told me to go home and practice giving enthusiastic thumbs-up in the mirror, I did it without question. When you asked me to present my experiences to other teachers, I did it without fear. I knew that your trust and faith in me would guide me toward a life fulfilled—and it has.

To my colleagues: Without you there would be fewer laugh lines, fewer gray hairs, fewer tears wiped gently from my cheeks, fewer stories, and far too few memories. I have been in education in some capacity for two decades. I have worked with thousands of amazing educators from prekindergarten to doctoral school. You continue to inspire me, amaze me, and push me to be more. This book is written with every hope that your work will inspire future teacher leaders.

To my husband and family who watch my ongoing battle with my personal academic demons: Thank you. Your belief in me is empowering. When I revert back to that first-grader who lives so strongly in my core, I pull from your vision of me to gain back my strength. Thank you, and I love you.

Most importantly, to each of you new teachers, experienced teachers, pondering teachers, struggling teachers, teacher-of-the-year teachers, wondering-if-you-can-do-this-another-day teachers: You are everything. You are strong and skilled and able to handle the bad days and the good days. I hope that this book finds you in a place of peace and kindness. I hope that there are lessons learned and strategies gained. We are a band of teachers, a brother and sisterhood of lifelong learners and compassionate givers. Keep up the great work.

Introduction

What is a happy class? A happy class begins with a happy teacher. A happy teacher is part of a happy school community. The classroom, the teacher, and the school help to cultivate happy and successful students.

In times of increased standardization and compliance, it is vital to refocus on positivity and individualization. Each student who walks through the schoolhouse doors has talent, skill, drive, ability, and possibility. Sometimes it can be hard to find—hidden under layers of struggle, challenges, trauma, or fear—but it is all there. Children are born to learn. Humans are wired to make ongoing neural connections. The brain is malleable and trainable.

This book is intended to share strategies to help create or regain a happy class.

- If you are a *new teacher*, there are tips and strategies to help set up a classroom for success and start from the ground up.
- If you are an *experienced teacher*, there are ideas for tweaks and twists to help build on what you already have in place.
- If you are an *administrator*, there are ideas of what to look for on walkthroughs, in professional-learning communities, or during meetings.
- If you are *support staff*, there are techniques to help build strong relationships with colleagues and connect interdisciplinary work in meaningful ways.

A happy class requires a happy teacher. Happy teachers feel empowered to address challenging behavior. Happy teachers believe that *every* child can learn. Happy teachers believe that families and caregivers are doing the best that they can with what they have. Happy teachers recognize the stress in themselves and others and find healthy coping strategies. Happy teachers balance work and outside life. Happy teachers are compassionate and empathetic. Most of all, happy teachers are happiest when they are teaching.

Each chapter of this book is designed to help focus your energy and work toward creating a happy class. This is done through using organizational strategies, understanding human behavior, developing strategies for challenging behavior and interventions focused on success, utilizing positive supports, using the right data to help make decisions, and also, keeping yourself healthy and happy.

Ultimately, each chapter should lead you on a journey of self-discovery. Each strategy should guide you toward being strengths-based, focusing on the good in each person and each situation. In order to be a happy teacher with a happy class, you may need to make personal adjustments; that is okay. No one is perfect. Perfection is not the goal; happiness is. That happiness is defined by you but shared with everyone you interact with. Your happiness should be contagious.

Consider reading through this book quickly the first time. Take one strategy that you learned and apply it in your classroom for a period of time. Take notes on what works and what doesn't. Make adjustments. Read the book again and add another strategy and another until you feel you have built a strong foundation for a happy class.

Then read it again. Read it after winter and spring breaks. Read it after summer break and before the start of a new school year. Read it when things are not working well, and read it when they are. Share the strategies with colleagues. Add the ideas to lesson plans and individual plans. Read when you need motivation, and read it when you need validation.

Read it to ensure you have a happy class.

Chapter One

Organizing for Happiness

ORGANIZING FOR YOU

The first step to a happy classroom is being organized for success. With the demands of ongoing instruction and assessment there is often little wiggle room in the day for extra time. In order to maximize time and ensure that learning can happen from bell to bell, it is crucial to be well organized and well prepared.

Start with your desk or personal area. Even if you have to fake it until you make it, clean up your area. If an expectation is that student materials are tidy and put away, you'll need to model that. Start by getting some organizational tools such as decorative baskets, pencil holders, binders, crates, and bins. A visit to your local resale or donation store can help to save some money on these items. Have a personal bookshelf with space for containers, binders, teaching materials, and personal items. Great teaching happens away from the desk, so have necessary items within reach and strategically placed throughout the classroom. Small containers of writing utensils, extra notepads, and student rewards can be placed around the room.

Create specific locations for different teaching and learning opportunities. For example, if you use one consistent location for whole-group instruction, students will learn the expectations for that location more quickly because of the consistent routine. You can organize the classroom into sections or spaces to create simple boundaries for activities. For example, a small table can be used for small-group instruction. A nook can be created in the classroom for special activities. Secondary students can use a designated nook area to work on projects.

Consider the theme and color of your overall classroom design. The classroom can be decorated with the school mascot, a specific color scheme or based on student group names (e.g., animal types, colors, character traits, etc.). For some students and adults, too much color can feel chaotic and uncomfortable. Create a theme and stick to it. Determine one to two calming colors and find or create containers, materials, and decorations that complement the color theme. Blues and purples have been known to have calming effects, whereas reds and yellows are associated with hunger and eating. Be strategic with your design scheme based on your student's needs. You may need to keep decorations on the walls to a minimum to support focus on the instructor.

Have a filing cabinet or filing baskets for past lesson plans that you can easily access. You can also organize these electronically if you create consistent file names. You'll want to save meeting agendas, meeting notes, parent contacts, and any professional development sessions that you attend, either in print or electronic files.

ORGANIZING FOR OTHERS

As a teacher, you work with a number of great professionals. You may co-teach classes or have teachers pushing into the classroom or pulling out of the classroom. You may have instructional assistants, teaching partners, intern teachers, or paraprofessionals providing support. It can be helpful to organize the classroom for their success as well.

One of the most overlooked components to working effectively with teaching partners is common planning. You may need to advocate for time to co-plan with the other teachers who support your classroom. If that isn't possible, find alternatives like e-mail strands, live-streaming apps for smartphones or computers, or document programs that allow for multiple participants. As the teacher you are responsible for creating and designing the instruction, but when it comes to effectively teaching all students, it is all hands on deck.

Another important piece to working with teaching partners is the creation of meaningful relationships. After all, these are teaching *partners*. Having a partner implies that you are part of a teaching relationship. Relationships often take conscious effort and work. Begin by creating a set of norms and values. Review your common beliefs about learning, achievement, and student goals. Determine specific roles for each partner. Create plans for including teaching partners in activities, meetings, discussions, learning communities, planning, assessment, and so forth (see table 1.1).

As a teacher you will also work with a number of professional collaborators. Most schools have social workers, school psychologists, school counselors, outside agency representatives, school nurses, volunteers, and others who will be available to provide assistance in the classroom. People in those roles may be helping to support students with special needs, they may help implement academic or behavioral plans, or they may consult with you on classroom management strategies or instructional techniques.

Table 1.1.   Example of a Shared Teaching Responsibility Plan

Task/Activity	Teacher Responsibility	Teaching Partner Responsibility	Shared Responsibility
Planning			
Assessment			
Instruction			
Progress Monitoring			
Classroom Management			
Meetings/Committees			
Family Communication			

To help organize those supports, have clear schedules for lessons and activities. If there are changes to the schedule, create a communication plan for support staff. This can be as easy as e-mailing or text-messaging your teaching partners where you'll be and when you'll be there. This way, a social worker who needs to pull a student out to provide individual counseling, for example, will know the best times and places to do so.

Another thing to consider when working with professional collaborators is organizing for meetings. One of the realities of teaching is that there are a lot of meetings to attend, facilitate, and plan for. Before a meeting, communicate to those invited or involved the purpose of the meeting, possible talking points, and any materials, items, or ideas that they should have ready. Create an agenda and e-mail it out to all involved prior to the meeting. For expected difficult or contentious meetings, consider pre-meeting to role-play difficult conversations. As the teacher it may be your responsibility to facilitate the meeting and help teams come to consensus.

Tips for Gaining Consensus

- Understand that consensus is not about 100 percent agreement; it is that, in general, the group as a whole agrees that something is an issue or an action plan is needed.
- Have a list of meeting/discussion norms and an agenda to keep everyone on the same page and help guide conversations back to the main concern or topic.
- Make attempts to hear from all parties involved (through round-robin format, written input, or small-group conversations).
- Discuss any points of disagreement and create a list of the items that everyone can agree on.
- Refrain from voting or creating "teams" by hearing all stakeholder input (including families, if involved), validating that input, and including components of each person's input into a final action plan.

- If someone continues to be in disagreement, document that participant's concerns in a way that satisfies him or her (in meeting minutes, on school letterhead, or in the action or intervention plan).
- Recognize that gaining consensus may require multiple meetings and ongoing discussion.

ORGANIZING FOR A SUBSTITUTE

As a classroom teacher there is no more important person to organize for than a substitute teacher. When developing and planning your lessons, a great tip is to have a friend or family member read through it. If your friends or family members had to spend a day in your classroom, could they follow your lesson plan? Most of the time a substitute is needed because the teacher is ill or has some other emergency. If you are not ready for those circumstances, your substitute can be lost and a day's worth of learning lost with it.

Create a substitute-teacher binder. In the front pocket of the binder include any classroom passes that students may need, tickets or stickers for your classroom management token economy, and maybe some special treats that a substitute could hand out. Include pages for the school's emergency procedures, a student roster, the bus and walker list, school contacts, and daily schedule. Include a list of student-specific information. Who needs extra attention or has other special needs, allergies, specific plans, alternative schedules, and so forth? Who are the go-to helpers? You can even include student learning-style preferences. Include a section for extension activities or material to help fill any gaps in the day. These may be word puzzles, a list of websites that students can visit, or previous work that students can catch up on. You can add your daily lesson plans as needed.

In the back of the binder, add two template letters. One letter should be a thank-you from you to the substitute. The second should be a fillable template that the substitute can fill out to you. Include space to write in what was accomplished during the day and what parts of lessons may not have been completed. Have lines for the substitute to write which students were helpers and which students needed help. Allow the substitute to share his or her reflections on the day. This simple step can be crucial to establishing a good relationship with substitutes and may help to secure consistent subs for your classroom.

ORGANIZING FOR STUDENTS

The classroom is a great place to start. Traditional classrooms with rows of tidy wooden desks are a thing of the past. Today the focus is on authentic learning and education that meets all learners' needs, including different learning modalities. In organizing the space in your classroom, consider your last trip to the grocery store. Grocery stores are very intentionally designed. In fact, larger retailers often consult with behavioral and social psychologists to understand consumer behavior. Designs are intentionally planned to meet everyone's needs and to encourage specific behaviors. Items are placed strategically. Colors are chosen with care. Accessibility for all is part of the design.

Now picture your classroom. Designing for all learners is a process derived from the concept of architectural design. The grocery store has ramps for persons in wheelchairs, highly purchased items are easily accessible, soft music may be playing in the background, and colors are bright and inviting. The classroom design should be as thoughtful. Would a wheelchair easily pass through the aisles and open areas in your classroom? Is the classroom easy on all five senses (lights are not overwhelming, sounds are not too loud, textures are not irritating)? Can students of all sizes and ages access necessary materials?

Simple changes can make a tremendous difference. For instance, if students will be engaging in collaborative work, consider arranging desks in groups of three or four with organization tools at each grouping (figure 1.1).

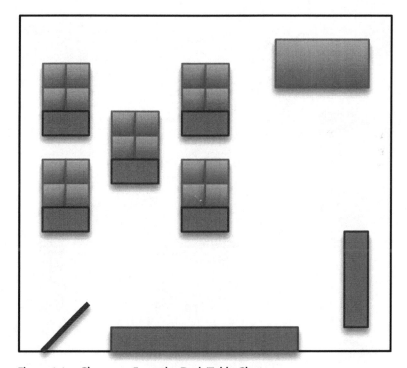

Figure 1.1.   Classroom Example: Desk/Table Clusters

Organization tools can be small bookshelves with binders, writing tools, and books. Materials can also be organized in transportable totes at each grouping of desks. Small groups of desks or groups of students around smaller tables will encourage conversation and collaboration.

If students will primarily be doing active and kinesthetic learning desks or tables can be arranged along the perimeter of the class so that activities can occur in the center (figure 1.2). Perimeter seating can also be organized in small clusters to encourage group work. Perimeter seating can be beneficial to create rotating centers for activity work as well.

For instructional learning, the classroom can be organized as a semicircle (figure 1.3). This arrangement allows for the instructor to easily move from student to student and to utilize proximity control. The semicircle can also include a center table that creates a fishbowl for learning. As the semicircle is working on individual activities, a small group can be getting additional instruction at the fishbowl table.

All of the examples above encourage different types of interaction between teacher and learner and between students. An important concept is to con-

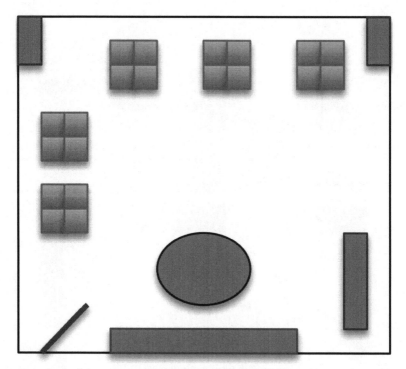

Figure 1.2.   Classroom Example: Perimeter Seating

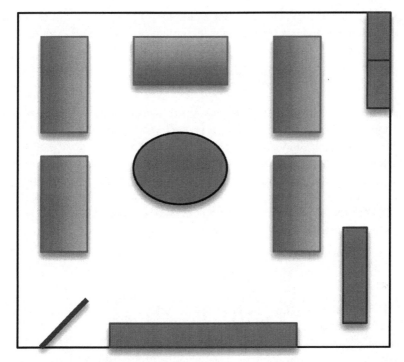

Figure 1.3.   Classroom Example: Semicircle

sider having multiple learning areas within a classroom. Each arrangement described above can also create space for specific activities. You may want to include a calming area that includes activities to support sensory needs and self-regulation. Some items to include in a calming area are soft seating, stress balls, a timer, coloring pages, relaxing music, softer lighting.

Another important organizational need is preparing for learning through lesson plans. Some schools and districts may have required lesson-planning templates. If not, there are plenty of great template examples online. The important piece of lesson-planning organization is knowing that the more time you put into designing the lesson for all learners, the more time you'll have to focus on teaching the lesson. It is difficult to invest the up-front time for lesson planning, but in the end it truly pays off.

Ensure that when creating your lessons, you are including multiple modalities. Do a learning-style inventory with your students early in the year and ensure that each lesson incorporates aspects of each learning preference (verbal, visual, musical, physical, logical). Simple and quick learning-style inventories can easily be found online. Even when curricula are scripted or have required elements, add extension activities that will help match learner styles and increase engagement. For example, a scripted reading lesson can be extended for students by adding role-playing or sequencing activities.

CHAPTER SUMMARY

There are many ways to be more organized and prepared in the classroom. Keep in mind that the ultimate goal is student success and determine the best ways to help your students succeed by considering their environment and classroom structure. Remember that you are the model for their organizational behaviors. In what ways can you model good organizational strategies and help teach them strategies as well? In addition, you'll be working with a number of other professionals, and organization can help make those relationships more successful and efficient.

REFLECTION QUESTIONS

Q1. In your classroom you have three students who are pulled out for a related service (occupational therapy, speech therapy, physical therapy). You have one student who has an instructional aide, and you have a social worker who comes in twice a week to do a social skills group. How will you organize a schedule that includes those professionals? What changes need to be made to your current schedule?

Q2. You have a meeting next week with a family who has been challenging to work with in the past. The family members are strong advocates for their student, who is currently underperforming academically. You'd like the school counselor and social worker to attend the meeting and provide input, but you have no time to meet in advance. What strategies can you use to prepare for the meeting?

Q3. Your current classroom is a collection of "antique" inspirational posters. You haven't updated your décor in several years. How can you make minor adjustments to the décor in the room to support student learning?

Q4. Make a list of all the strategies that help you feel organized in your home and personal life. How can those effective strategies be applied to your teaching/work life?

Chapter Two

Everything You Need to Know, You Can Learn from a Kindergarten Teacher

ESTABLISHING CLASSROOM RULES AND POSSIBLE OUTCOMES

It has likely been a long time since you have been in kindergarten. If you haven't been in a kindergarten classroom in a while, then you really should visit one soon. Kindergarten classrooms are like well-oiled machines. There is little downtime, high amounts of structure, and a lot of happy, positive, and consistent feedback. Whether your students are five or fifteen, the lessons of a kindergarten classroom can be applied at all levels.

Clear and well-established academic and behavioral expectations are necessary for a happy classroom. If your school already has school-wide expectations or a clear vision, you can use that as a starting point for your classroom rules. For example, if the school expects students to be respectful and responsible, your classroom rules can describe what that looks like in the classroom. If the school has a vision of creating concerned citizens, your classroom rules can specify what classroom behaviors are required (see table 2.1).

Classroom rules should describe the specific behaviors that are necessary for students to be successful. Take the concept of being respectful as an example. Respect is a very broad construct and can mean different things to different people. To be more specific for classroom rules, respect may look like students interacting with all students using school-appropriate language. Being responsible may look like students having materials ready for instructional time.

Classroom rules should be stated positively. Many times teachers create rules that say what *not* to do. This can be confusing for students. If the rules are focused on what to do, it will be easier to teach the behaviors and reward students for following the rules. It is easy to see when students have their

Table 2.1. Procedures for Arrival, Dismissal, and Transitions

Expectations and Rules Matrix	
School Expectations	*Classroom Rules*
Be Safe.	• Keep all four legs of chairs on the floor. • Use walking feet. • Follow equipment instructions when in use.
Be Respectful.	• Use school-appropriate language. • Treat all people with kindness and compassion. • Listen when others are speaking.
Be Responsible.	• Arrive to class on time. • Have materials ready. • Ask questions.

materials ready for an activity. It is easy to identify students who are using school-appropriate language with each other. Instead of "don't run in the aisles," the rule can be stated positively as "use walking feet in the classroom at all times."

No matter the age range of a particular class, one great way to create the list of rules is to create it together as a class. This strategy will provide students with ownership over the classroom and the expected behaviors. You'll need to determine what the nonnegotiable rules are. Then you can create a lesson plan that allows for you and the students to negotiate and create additional rules as a class.

A good guideline for rule-making is to keep the number of rules between three and five. That may seem overwhelming. How can you pair down your list of rules to less than six? It's actually quite simple. Most classroom rules are repetitive. For instance, "don't call out," "raise your hand," and "wait for the teacher" can all be lumped into a rule of "raise a quiet hand and wait for the teacher to respond." Go through your current rules and organize them into themes; then create a positively stated rule for the theme. This will help to focus on three to five positively stated, specific rules to help students know exactly what is expected of them.

The other component to classroom rules is classroom outcomes. Most people call outcomes "consequences." You will learn in chapter 4 that the term *consequence* does not equal what happens when a rule is broken. What should happen after a rule is broken is *discipline*. Discipline is focused on teaching and facilitating learning. So an outcome of breaking a rule may result in re-learning the rule or behavior. It may result in creating an intervention plan or engaging in a behavior of repairing any harm to the person or environment. It may result in a traditional negative outcome like an office referral.

When you are creating your classroom rules, you also want to create an outcome hierarchy. What are the tiers of support that will be provided to students when a rule is broken? In later chapters, you will learn more about effective consequences based on the challenging behavior that is being observed, but for the sake of creating a general outcome hierarchy, there are several tips to consider.

The outcome hierarchy should be tiered or scaffolded so that students have an opportunity to continue toward success. No classroom should have a "strike out" policy. You want students to have opportunities to relearn and refocus toward learning.

A first step in the hierarchy may include a reminder about the rule and expected behavior. This reminder should include some reteaching and role-playing or practice opportunity. A second step may be contacting the parent. A good policy for contacting parents is to be sure to contact them regularly with positive reports, so that when you have to call for a behavioral concern, you have already developed a strong pattern of information-sharing. You can actually schedule positive phone calls home each week to help build parent partnerships. This way, you are not calling parents *only* when there is not-so-good news.

Based on your school's policies, a third step may be an individual intervention support. This may look like a behavioral agreement or goal for success for the rest of the day or an individual or small-group social skill lesson related to the behavior. In chapters 3 and 5 you will learn much more about aligning interventions to the function of the behavior and to specific challenging behaviors.

What you want to be cautious of is using outcomes that are not effective. Strategies like time out, office referrals, and suspension should be used cautiously and based on student need and behavior. A good gauge for effectiveness is that if you have to use a certain outcome procedure on a regular basis, over and over, it is not effectively changing the challenging behavior. Another outcome procedure should probably be considered.

In some kindergarten classes you may see an outcome strategy of color charts being used. These certainly have their place, but they may need some tweaking to be effective in your classroom. Consider yourself as a student who talked out of turn in class. You are asked to go to the color-clip chart and move your clip to red, or you are called out in front of your friends. You are embarrassed not only because your enthusiasm to answer the question overtook your knowledge of the classroom rule to raise your hand before speaking, but also because you have to parade in front of the entire class and fortify everyone's belief that you are a challenging student and classmate. Plus, it is only nine o'clock, or first period, and you are already on red, that is, you have already had to try to save face in front of your peers. What is the point of behaving appropriately the rest of the day?

For most students the color-clip chart process can create anxiety, stigmatization, and actualization of perceptions about behavior and esteem. However, the clip chart can be a useful tool in the classroom with a few minor changes. The system can also be broadened and updated to work across all grade levels.

One easy update is to adjust the number of colors. Rather than the obvious green, yellow, and red, consider using more neutral colors or a wider array of colors. Align the colors to your classroom colors. This will create less automatic responses to the stoplight perception that red equals bad. It is more important to teach students how to behave than to only imply that they need to stop behaving.

Another easy adjustment is to include in the system an opportunity for elementary students to move back to favorable levels so that a clip move is not a *full day* penalty. You can also start in a neutral zone and students can move up and down throughout the day. In a secondary classroom period, you can include more opportunities to turn the behavior around. When establishing your classroom rules with your students, be clear about how they can earn back their favorable standing and how quickly that can occur. This will encourage students to persevere behaviorally and academically in the classroom.

Still, a chart system is not a necessary classroom management system. Later chapters, especially 3, 4, and 5, will help you to create more effective strategies and updates to your classroom management system. Other ideas and more functional and logical consequences—more positive responses to challenging behavior—will be described. If you are committed to a color chart or as a secondary teacher you use other systems, consider some simple adjustments. If you are willing to try something new, think about more function-based intervention strategies.

UTILIZING INSTRUCTIONAL TIME AND TIMELY TRANSITIONS: CHOCOLATE TO CHOCOLATE

One of the most challenging times in most classes is the downtime that can occur between lessons and activities. It is vital to plan from bell to bell. The old adage that idle hands are more likely to find trouble often proves true. Again, picture the kindergarten classroom. There are timers to indicate when a transition is going to occur. There are visual and verbal prompts and instructions provided to know how to transition. Materials are ready in areas that are being transitioned to. There are songs about transitioning to help create a smooth process. Students are rewarded for getting to their area on time and being ready to learn.

These are all strategies that are helpful at any age and developmental level. They may be adjusted, but what works for a five-year-old is often a strategy that will work for a fifteen-year-old. Designing your instruction is one important component to utilizing instructional time effectively, but transition time can eat away at instructional time.

Speaking of eating, what does chocolate have to do with classroom transitions? Chocolate may be a survival food for many teachers, but it's also a great strategy to help smooth a rough transition routine. You may be a big fan of vegetables. They are necessary for a healthy diet. But have you ever experienced having a child eat dessert first and then asking him or her to eat vegetables? It is not very likely that children will eat a candy bar and then be ready for a big plate of carrots and green beans.

The same concept applies to transitions. Most students wouldn't prefer to go from an engaging activity to a stagnant lecture. Students often have difficulty moving from high-energy classes like physical education to quiet listening for math or reading. Instead of creating transitions that go from chocolate to broccoli, create transitions that go from chocolate to chocolate.

Not all chocolate is the same. Have you ever stood in a grocery store candy aisle? There is baker's chocolate, semi-sweet chocolate, milk chocolate, 70 percent cacao, and chocolate with every imaginable morsel added to it. When you are building your day and planning your lessons, you want to consider what kind of chocolate is the right one. As an example, writing is often a challenging task for students. If your lesson plan includes whole group instruction in writing—which is comparable to broccoli or even cabbage or lima beans for some students—then add some hot fudge to the day with an activity that includes movement and creativity.

If you use centers or stations in an elementary classroom, they can't all be milk chocolate, or else the students would get a bellyache after the second station and not want to continue in the following stations. Instead, mix up the stations to address multiple learning styles. For example, students could go from an action station to a listening station and then to a creative station. In a secondary classroom, there may be rotations of whole-group, small-group, and independent work.

When in doubt, sandwich it out. If you know that you have to move from a highly preferred activity to one that may be less preferred, let the students know that something fun is embedded into the lesson. For instance, if the daily schedule has language arts after music or art, which are typically more preferred classes, then create a lesson plan that includes a highly engaging, culminating activity. Some ideas might be acting out letter sounds, re-creating an older play in modern times, or interpreting text by drawing or dancing.

It's also good to build in some broccoli-to-chocolate moments. In behavior analysis, this strategy is called the Premack Principle,[1] Grandma's Law, or First-Then. Chapter 5 provides more specifics of when and how to use the Premack Principle. The concept works by pairing a less preferred activity with a more preferred activity. The more preferred activity acts as the reward for having completed the less preferred activity. Eventually, with enough pairing, students may even begin to like the less preferred activity because they know something more fun follows. If they eat their broccoli knowing that they can have chocolate when they're done, even a stubborn child may start to like broccoli.

LOST AND FORGOTTEN PROCEDURES

Like transitions, attention signals are also an important part of effective classroom routines. An attention signal can include a visual prompt like switching the lights on and off or a verbal prompt such as "eyes on me" or "three, two, one." Some teachers may even use an actual bell. When you deliver a transition prompt, do so in one specific place in the classroom or hallway. This is your transition prompting spot. This area should only be used for the attention signal and not for instruction. When you are waiting for the students to respond to the signal, wait silently so that you are modeling the appropriate behavior. This may take patience and practice at first, but eventually students will pick up on the routine.

Students will quickly learn that when you are standing in the attention signal area they need to wait for instructions for the next activity. Soon, when you start walking toward that area of the classroom, the students will begin to quiet down and await directions. This process is referred to as stimulus control.

"Withitness" is another aspect of a happy class and happy teacher. Strong withitness will help with classroom routines and procedures. Withitness is the concept of teachers being aware of what is going on with all students within the classroom. Having good withitness means that you quickly respond to needs and take action to address classroom behaviors. You are able to triage needs when there are multiple students in need of assistance. You can effectively address challenging behavior before it becomes disruptive. Most importantly you can do all of this without interfering with ongoing instruction.

Withitness requires that you can easily see and move around all areas of the classroom and actively scan the classroom on a regular basis to assess needs and engagement. Some teachers will create routines for how to ask questions in a way that it is not disruptive. Strategies may include having colored cards on student desks to indicate their need for assistance, as follows:

- Green means they can do the activity without assistance.
- Yellow means that they need help but it's not an emergency.
- Red means that they can't begin work until they get more assistance.

Another strategy is having a designated area in the classroom where students can post or ask questions. If you have one in the classroom, a smart board can assist in organizing student questions. You can also write them out on a whiteboard, text them to students, or have them on sticky notes on students' desks. The most important piece is to prioritize student needs to encourage active engagement in the activity.

Table 2.2 provides a list of the procedures that should be in every classroom along with tips for how it may be accomplished.

Table 2.2.   Classroom Procedure Considerations.

Procedures for Arrival, Dismissal, and Transitions	
Entering the classroom	Greet students by name at the door; orient students to expected work or behaviors.
Dismissing at the end of the period or day	Use a timed warning system prior to the end of the day or class (ten-, five-, two-minute warnings).
Returning to class after an absence	Use a folder or filing system to orient students to make up work, hand in any completed work, and request assistance for missed work; establish a clear timeline for makeup work and include in your grading policy.
Arriving to class tardy	Assign each student a work buddy to help orient to work/task/activity; create time to review any instruction missed; create system for homework if activity is missed and requires makeup.
Beginning of the period or day	Create a "bell work" routine that consistently requires students to engage in a starting task (this may be the first scaffold of learning for the lesson); post the bell work in an easily visible and accessible area.
Asking for help; asking questions	Use a card or clipboard system to help triage questions based on need; create a timeline for responses (if a quiet hand is raised, the teacher will respond within 30 seconds); use visual cues and active student responding throughout lesson as formative assessment to gauge understanding.
Lining up; going to specials or the library	Call students by name or group to help with the flow of lining up; for younger students, have specifically defined area to stand during lineup process (tape marks or feet stickers) to help with spacing; rotate line positions regularly; review expectations for

(continued)

Table 2.2. (*continued*)

Procedures for Arrival, Dismissal, and Transitions	
Lining up; going to specials or the library	hallway behavior prior to entering the hallway; have a lineup song that helps with timing of transition
Preparing for lunch	Use a timed warning system prior to lunchtime (ten-, five-, two-minute warnings); review lunchroom expectations prior to entering the lunchroom.
Attendance	Follow policies when they are defined by a school or district. Otherwise, create system to contact/notify parents if attendance is impacting performance; work with families to establish routines that will assist with attendance (students can set alarms/reminders on phone, provide calendar of important events, use online planner or website to notify of important assignments/work).

Whole-Group, Small-Group, and Independent Instructional Activities	
Working cooperatively	Explicitly teach expected collaboration behaviors; define specific roles for students within groups (i.e., notetaker, timekeeper, spokesperson); group students strategically based on the task (refrain from only using skill-/level-based grouping); create areas in the classroom that are conducive to group work (grouped tables/desks).
Finding directions for each assignment	Post directions in easily visible/accessible areas; post directions in small steps; chunk lessons so directions can be broken into smaller steps; for missed or makeup assignments, include directions in a binder or folder for makeup work.
Collecting/returning student work	Use a bin or mailbox system for work; in- and out-boxes could be placed at each desk or a specified area of the classroom by period/subject grouping (in-box is for upcoming/daily work, out-box is for turning in assignments); create a classroom job/responsibility for work collector and distributor.
Having materials ready	Have materials for each lesson easily accessible for tables or table groups; post necessary materials in an easily accessible location (on the board or online page).
Passing out materials	Create a classroom job/responsibility for material manager; have necessary materials already placed in the activity areas.
Heading work	Create a consistent system for titling work (name, date, period/subject); teach a process (last name_date_subject/period) of name logic for electronic work.

Whole-Group, Small-Group, and Independent Instructional Activities	
Dealing with unfinished work	Determine if unfinished work will become required homework; create a time during the week that unfinished work can be completed; have a space for unfinished work to be kept until it can be completed (mailbox, filing system, binder, notebook).
Managing early completers	Plan for early completers by including extension/ enrichment activities in the lesson plan; post activities that can be done when finished (read a book, color/write, complete other work); review expectations for early finishers when delivering activity instructions.
Being a classroom helper or learning a classroom responsibility	Define classroom roles/responsibilities; create a rotation process that allows for each person to access a job/responsibility; focus jobs toward student strengths/interests; explicitly teach and model the behaviors of that responsibility.
Helping peers	Strategically assign classroom buddies who students can request help from; create a classroom responsibility of resource finder/helper; create time in lessons for peer work and collaboration.
Breaks and Downtime	
When and how to use the restroom	Create a restroom pass and the number of times that pass can be used in a certain time period; be mindful and accepting of restroom emergencies; teach explicitly the expectation for time away from instruction; post proper restroom behaviors and etiquette visibly in the restroom.
When and how to use the drinking fountain or sink	Create a sink/fountain pass and the number of times that pass can be used in a certain time period; be mindful and accepting of sink/fountain emergencies; teach explicitly the expectation for time away from instruction; post proper fountain/ sink behaviors and etiquette visibly near the water fountain and/or sink.
When and how to use the pencil sharpener	Create a pencil pass and the number of times that pass can be used in a certain time period; be mindful and accepting of pencil emergencies (have pencils available for students to use); teach explicitly the expectation for time away from instruction; post proper pencil sharpener behaviors and etiquette visibly near the pencil sharpener.

(continued)

Table 2.2. *(continued)*

	Breaks and Downtime
Throwing away trash/ recycling	Have small trash bins near table/desk groupings; have multiple trash receptacles throughout the classroom; post proper trash and recycling behaviors and etiquette visibly near the receptacles; explicitly teach about recycling and garbage; create a classroom waste management responsibility.
When and how to get to locker	Create a locker pass and the number of times that pass can be used in a certain time period; be mindful and accepting of emergencies; teach explicitly the expectation for time away from instruction; post proper locker use behaviors and etiquette visibly near lockers.

	Other Things that Routinely Happen in the Classroom
Lost and Found items	Create a space in the classroom for lost and found items; determine if the school has a process in place for lost and found items; create a classroom responsibility for monitoring for, collecting, and determining what to do with lost and found items.
Classroom visitors	Make all attempts to notify students in advance if visitors are expected; discuss with visitors prior to arrival any expectations or information that may be important; review the classroom rules with students regarding expected behaviors; create time for classroom visitors to interact with students at a time that does not directly interfere with instruction.
Organizing and cleaning up area	Set a timer with a specific amount of time to help with the effectiveness of cleaning up; explicitly review what is required for cleaning up and/or organizing; create time in the week to do a classroom cleanup; have the plant operator deliver a lesson on cleaning up the classroom.

CHAPTER SUMMARY

Designing and delivering lessons are major job responsibilities of the classroom teacher. Instructional time is highly coveted and necessary to ensure that lessons and assessments are completed based on specific scopes and sequences. Transitions, routines, and procedures in the classroom can help to minimize downtime and effectively use instructional time. By considering all of the possible procedures that may be needed, you can better prepare the classroom. By planning and preparing for effective transitions and minimizing downtime, you can create a happier class that is able to focus on the tasks at hand.

REFLECTION QUESTIONS

Q1. Your administrator has informed you that he or she will be coming into your classroom next week to conduct classroom observations. You have lesson plans ready but want to be sure that the students are ready for this type of observation. What strategies can you use to prepare your students for the administrator's classroom walkthroughs?

Q2. It is the middle of the school year and you have not yet established classroom jobs or responsibilities. What would be a few classroom jobs that you could start with to help with classroom procedures?

Q3. You have a lesson plan ready for tomorrow that includes some activities that may not be highly preferred by students. They are required, district-scripted lessons with assessments. Last time the students were not engaged and struggled to transition to the next activity. How can you adjust the activity before or after the required district lesson to encourage a better transition and engagement?

Q4. Your teaching partner currently has fifteen classroom rules. Many of them are stated in the negative. Your classroom rules have been slimmed down to four and they are positively stated. How can you work with your teaching partner to help create a more effective set of classroom rules?

NOTE

1. D. Premack, "Reversibility of the Reinforcement Relation," *Science*, New Series 136, no. 3512 (April 20, 1962): 255–57.

Chapter Three

Function Junction

Why Does This Keep Happening?
Understanding the Functions of Behavior

For practical purposes, it is important to understand the four basic functions of behavior. So, let's take a trip into Function Junction.

The *function of a behavior* really just means that we need to understand *why* a behavior is occurring. Once we understand the *why*, we'll be able to build better interventions. If we don't understand the *why* (the function), then we'll likely be working ourselves and the students in circles. In many cases, people give up on behavior analytic practices because what they attempt is not successful for any number of reasons, but most often because they have not identified the correct function of a given behavior.

All behavior occurs for some reason. No one truly does anything "out of the blue." We typically engage in a behavior because we get an outcome that we like. We may get a smile back when we smile casually at a stranger in the grocery store, so we'll likely smile kindly at the next stranger as well, hoping for the same outcome.

When we're thirsty and craving caffeine, we'll put our $1.25 into the soda machine, push the big soda button, and listen as the can clinks to the bottom. The next time we're thirsty, we'll go to the same soda machine that worked for us last time. If we don't want to get wet in the rain, we'll put up a hood or an umbrella each time we see sprinkles. If we don't like loud noises or crowds of people, we'll avoid going to certain places.

We do those things over and over because we like the payoff. We like the attention of nice, happy people. We like to avoid angry, mean people.

Consider this scenario: Melissa, a student in your class, calls out every time you begin to ask a question, whether she knows the answer or not. The calling out is often disruptive to you and the other students, and it makes it hard to get through a lesson. Sometimes, as a response to her calling out, you'll give her verbal reprimands, use proximity by standing by her desk, or maybe even send her to the office to speak to an administrator about her behavior. The calling out happens over and over throughout the day to the point where you become frustrated and even raise your voice.

Now consider this: Melissa lives in a home with six other siblings. Her mom is often busy with two jobs and her father is not available to assist with family issues. The siblings are often busy and do not give her much attention at home. She loves attention and likes to be right.

When Melissa is in class, she wants nothing more than the adult attention that she isn't able to get at home. At school she has noticed that the teacher will say nice things to students, but it is often in passing and usually has a flat affect. But, when the teacher gets upset, she'll raise her voice, she'll stand next to the student, and she'll even flail her arms and lean in close.

Neither the student nor the teacher is doing these things consciously, but both have an impact on the continuation of what can sometimes be a challenging behavior. The student calls out because she is craving attention, and the teacher is inadvertently providing it by talking to her when she calls out, standing by her, or sending her to the principal. As teachers, it is our response to a student's maladaptive attempt to gain attention that we need to change. That's right, it is *our* response that needs to change.

FOUR FUNCTIONS OF BEHAVIOR

Let's first learn the four main functions of behavior so we can then learn some effective strategies to address challenging behavior that may occur in the classroom.

Attention

Attention, the "desire" or "intent" to have or gain a person's awareness, concentration, notice, or interest, is usually desired from a specific person or persons. The attention can be sought from adults or peers. You are more likely to see attention-seeking behavior in the presence of a person or persons, especially one or more who are "preferred." This function is most often person-specific, not location- or time-specific.

Classroom Example: Suzanne tells inappropriate jokes when her friends are seated next to her because her friends all laugh at her jokes.

Escape or Avoidance

Both reflect the "desire" or "intent" to remove oneself from a place or person's presence that is aversive or undesirable. Escape implies that the removal occurs during the event or in the presence of the person, while avoidance implies that the removal occurs prior to the undesired event or person's presence. This function is most often associated with a specific event, person, time, or request to engage in a non-preferred activity.

Classroom Example—Escape: Jimmy takes a long bathroom break each time writing activities are presented.

Classroom Example—Avoidance: Jimmy takes a long bathroom break just prior to scheduled writing time.

Tangible

This is the "desire" or "intent" to gain access to a preferred item or activity. *Tangible* is most often associated with something that one can hold/manipulate (toy, food, game, etc.). This function is most often associated with the absence of or removal of a preferred item or activity.

Classroom Example: Felicia cries, stomps her feet, and takes a toy car away from a peer or an e-reader off another student's desk.

Sensory Input

This is the "desire" or "intent" to either gain or remove sensory input (e.g., light, sound, touch, etc.). This function is not dependent on the presence of a person or event and will occur anytime or anywhere. This function may also occur more often if a person is experiencing a perceived stressor.

Classroom Example: Alexander hums and taps his pencil on his desk when it is quiet.

We already talked about an example of attention-seeking behavior. Let's get a clearer picture of the other functions in the classroom. Again, the foundation of effective change strategies begins with understanding why the challenging behavior is occurring.

EXPANDING CLASSROOM EXAMPLES

Escape and avoidance occur frequently in classrooms. As teachers, we ask students to engage in any number of non-preferred tasks throughout a day, such as "get out your math book" or "begin your morning writing work." Face it—all of our students can't like *all* of our lesson plans every day! We may see challenging behavior when a student has a skill deficit in an academic area. Let's walk through an example of escaping/avoiding a math worksheet.

It is 9:20 a.m. You make an announcement that the class will be transitioning to math in two minutes. Sarah, a second grade student, has been quiet and focused all morning during the creative writing lesson. You glance up and notice that she is out of her seat sharpening her pencil. She didn't raise her hand or ask permission.

You give her a verbal warning in accordance with your outcome hierarchy (we'll see examples of this later in the book). She promptly sits back in her seat, but begins talking with her neighbor at a level above an inside voice. You remind Sarah that she will have a time out if she continues to break the classroom rules. Sarah then sticks her tongue out at you. You quickly go over to Sarah and begin talking with her about her behavior.

The transition bell rings and most students know to open their math book and begin working on the next worksheet. Meanwhile, you and Sarah are going back and forth in conversation about her behavior. After five minutes, you remind Sarah to open her book and begin working on the decimal place worksheet.

What has happened here? Sarah has avoided the math worksheet for at least five minutes. If the lesson segment time is twenty minutes, that is a quarter of the instructional time that she has successfully avoided.

Now let's imagine that Sarah is stuck on a problem on the worksheet. Remember, she has a deficit in foundational math skills. Sarah begins singing loudly in the classroom and it is disrupting other students. You walk over and let Sarah know that she has a ten-minute time out for her violation of the classroom rules. Sarah huffs, moves to the back of the classroom, and you set a timer for ten minutes. When the timer rings and Sarah walks back to her seat, the transition timer rings as a reminder that math time is almost over. Sarah managed to avoid and then escape the non-preferred task of changing decimal points.

When the function is escape/avoid, typically students are trying to get away from something. When the function is tangible, most often students are trying to gain or get access to something. When we think about tangible as a function, the first thing that typically comes to mind is the more elementary example of a student wanting a preferred toy or a particular food item. In this next example, however, let's look at a secondary school example.

Tommy is a student who wants access to the perfect chair next to the perfect girl. He enters health class just before the bell rings and slides into a chair toward the back of the room. This is typically where he sits, because he thinks he won't be called on as much to answer questions. He's wrong about that!

As the bell rings, a new student enters. She is asked to introduce herself to the class, and then she promptly takes a seat near the teacher's desk in the front of the room. Tommy stares at her the rest of the class period and carefully watches to see if her next class is across the hall with him. When she does begin walking toward Mrs. Ashley's class across the hallway, Tommy immediately rushes into that room and attempts to take the seat next to the new girl. But Jimmy quickly sits down in that same seat.

Tommy and Jimmy begin a verbal altercation over who was there first and who the seat belongs to. None of this seems to impress the new girl, and Tommy ends up with neither the seat nor the girl but, instead, a discipline referral. Tommy didn't get what he wanted when he wanted it.

Sensory input is the function that is most often confusing for people. It is the only function where you are either trying to gain *or* remove something. It is easiest to understand in terms of the five senses. What happens when you have a mosquito bite? In most cases, if you feel a physiological need to itch, you will scratch to remove the itchy feeling. If you have a headache, you may take an aspirin to remove the painful sensation of the headache.

For example, some people like to have noise when they study or write, so when they sit down to begin a task, they will often gain access to sensory input by turning on the television or music. Conversely, there are also people who are unable to concentrate or focus when there is background noise. They will likely try to remove the sensory input by moving away from the sound source, putting on quieting earphones, or turning off the music.

In the classroom, we will see students who fidget, flap their hands, rub their clothing, pinch their skin, tap the desk, and so forth. The function of sensory input is typically brought on by some perceived physiological need. You will know if it is sensory because it will occur anytime, anyplace, and is not dependent on the presence of any person, activity, or item. In other words, you can feel the need to itch in a sterile room. It's automatic.

REPLACING THE CHALLENGING WITH WHAT WORKS: REPLACEMENT BEHAVIORS

Now that we have toured the station at Function Junction and you have a good grasp on understanding the *whys* of behavior—the functions—we'll need to mosey on over to the next stop. We need to know how to intervene, that is, how to address the challenging behavior and begin to make change. The most important lesson at this Function Junction stop is that we can't *make* anyone do anything. We are going to work on setting up the environment based on our understanding of why the behavior is occurring, so that we can either *increase* a behavior that we want to see (a replacement behavior) or *decrease* the challenging behavior.

We'll start with the replacement behavior. The goal is to substitute the challenging behavior with a more socially appropriate behavior that matches the same function and provides virtually the same outcome. In its simplest form, the action answers the question, "what is it that we want the student to be doing?"

Sounds easy, right? It should be if we consistently think about the function of the behavior. A student is calling out in class and we have identified that the function is attention. So what is it that we want the student to be doing? Your first response may be, "I want the student to stop calling out." Well, that is true, but what do we want him or her to *do*? A behavior is something that we do physically or verbally.

You may be thinking to yourself, "I want students to raise their hand!" Yes. Raising a hand is a behavior. Remember the function—I want them to raise their hand to be called on by the teacher, thereby getting *attention* for the socially appropriate replacement behavior. Ding! Ding! Ding! That's the best answer in this scenario.

There are so many instances where our best intentions inadvertently reinforce or reward and thereby *maintain* the challenging behavior. Think about the attention example with Melissa that we first discussed. The teacher had the best intentions of working with the student. Had she understood that the student was seeking to gain attention, however, the teacher's responses may have been different.

Replacement Behavior Classroom Examples

The trick to the behavior in the raising hand example above is that *you* the teacher have to be able to provide the attention that is being sought when the student engages in the replacement behavior. What do you think would happen if students raised their hand (the behavior we want), but were ignored by the teacher? They might get frustrated and act out or lose interest in trying to gain your attention and become disruptive by seeking to gain peer attention.

In this example, let's also examine the fact that raising one's hand is not a complicated behavior. Surely students are able to raise their hand—so why don't they just do that? Let's go back to Melissa, our student who is starved for attention. Her teacher didn't provide animated attention for *appropriate* behavior, but did so for inappropriate behavior. Which would you work harder for?

A replacement behavior for escape/avoidance would allow the student to be removed from a non-preferred task or person in a socially appropriate way. Consider this: If a student is avoiding writing tasks by having a meltdown (crying, yelling, throwing items) before writing time begins, how can the student appropriately avoid writing instead? I know . . . they have to write, right? Yes. They do.

Even as adults, though, we create our own replacement behaviors for non-preferred tasks. When you've been staring at the computer screen for too long and your eyes are starting to cross and the words just aren't forming anymore and you're beginning to become agitated, you stand up, stretch, walk away for a brief moment, refresh, and come back to the task at hand. You take a short break—the socially appropriate way to temporarily escape. For students, we can create break passes or cool-off cards that they can use to *temporarily* escape or avoid a task.

What about for the function of tangible, you ask? This one may seem a bit tougher, but again, think about the simplest terms. If a student is trying to gain access to a tangible item but is doing so by taking it away from someone else without permission, what is the socially appropriate way to access that item? Asking for it, right?

This brings up another valuable lesson that will be studied in a later chapter: All behavior is a form of communication. In many cases we teach a student the socially appropriate way to request what it is that they want. We have to understand the function, what *it* is that they want first, and then we can build the skills to identify when it is wanted and how to request it.

Sensory input is a bit more challenging because it is not dependent on outside intervention; remember, it can occur in a sterile room. However, there are strategies that we can use. For the student who fidgets, flaps hands, taps on the desk, and rubs clothing we can provide more socially appropriate sensory items. Velcro can be attached to the underside of the student's desk or table so that it is not visible and is potentially less stigmatizing for the student to use in front of peers. The student can quietly rub the soft or rough side of the Velcro strip to gain sensory input. The student could also carry a small token or item in a pocket, to rub when needed. Chronic fidgeters can have exercise cords tightly wrapped around the legs of their chairs so that they can bounce their legs or quietly tap their feet on the cord.

The important thing to remember when you are pulling into Function Junction is to identify *why* the behavior is occurring so that you find the functionally equivalent replacement behavior *and* understand what *your* response needs to be to help meet that functional need.

INTERVENTION STRATEGIES ALIGNED TO FUNCTION

A good, well-thought-out intervention to address challenging behavior needs to include a replacement behavior. There are other intervention strategies that can be used as well, some that can be put in place before a challenging behavior (preventative), and some that can be put in place afterward (reactive). If the function of the behavior is understood and considered, then multiple intervention strategies can be used. Below are a few more examples of ideas that can be implemented in the classroom.

Attention and Escape/Avoidance

When it comes to attention-seeking behavior, consider providing noncontingent attention throughout the day. To do so, you'll want to create a well-thought-out schedule of reinforcement.

For instance, if you know that a student seeks attention nearly every ten minutes throughout a day, you'll want to create a plan of providing attention more often than every ten minutes, maybe every five minutes. You can set a quiet timer on your phone or computer to remind you to check in with the student, look up and give a thumbs-up or wink, or ask a prompting question, such as "are you doing okay?" or "do you need any help?"

By providing attention on a regular basis you can avoid the student engaging in challenging behavior to receive that attention. Eventually, you'll want to spread that five minutes out to ten and then twenty, and then at some point the attention can be more random and periodic.

A student who commonly seeks attention may also benefit from being a class leader or having a classroom job. One strategy is to have the student work with classmates (especially if the student is motivated by peer attention) and to provide lots of positive praise to that student for performing the class job. The student can appropriately gain peer attention, peers can assist in the process and learn valuable empathy skills, and the whole class can benefit from the positive intervention.

You may also have a student who commonly tries to escape or avoid; this is a student who tries to get out of doing work or is a professional procrastinator. For the escape artist, one of the most practical strategies is to make learning engaging and meaningful. You can do this by gathering information about student learning styles, preferred topics of interest, and ability/skill levels, and incorporating that information into your planned lessons.

For instance, you can let a student who typically procrastinates have some choice of topic for a paper or writing assignment. You can turn assignments into games or friendly classroom competitions. You can also incorporate multiple learning styles when designing your lesson (a visual component, a movement component, an extension activity, etc.).

Another consideration is to combine easier tasks with more complicated tasks so that the work does not become overwhelming. Or you can provide opportunities for choice with regard to schedule or activities. Students may not be able to rearrange the time that Reading takes place, but perhaps within Reading they could choose to go to the listening station first and then read the passage. In a secondary classroom, students could have more choice in which part of the work to begin or different ways to complete the task (e.g., instead of writing a paper, they could create a presentation, poem, brochure, or song). You can also help the student to recognize when to plan or schedule small breaks before, during, or after tasks.

Remember, with escape-maintained behavior, the student must always complete the initial or requested task. If students are given the opportunity to escape once, they will likely do it again. So, if a student takes a break, she or he must be taught to go back, once the break is complete, to the original task or request and finish that task. It is necessary for students to know that even if they avoid or escape a task temporarily, the task doesn't go away.

Think about your own behavior. If you are working on a big project for work that has deadlines and maybe even consequences for not completing it, you can take short breaks when you get frustrated or you need to spend time with your family or watch your favorite reality TV show, but you still have to go back and complete it to meet your deadline.

TANGIBLE AND SENSORY INPUT: COMMUNICATION

When it comes to accessing preferred items, it makes sense that most people want what they want when they want it. But we have to learn how to ask for items appropriately. That is the most effective strategy to address the need to gain preferred items.

Teach students to communicate their wants and needs to others. Initially, that may not even be with words. For students who have difficulty communicating, consider having pictures of preferred items that they can use to request them. Technology can also be used in this instance. An e-reader or smartphone can be loaded with pictures or spoken requests for preferred items.

It is also important to utilize verbal praise when you observe students using the appropriate request or sharing preferred items with others. You also want to remember to ignore instances when the item is not requested appropriately, use a verbal reminder of how to ask for the item, and then provide the item when it is requested appropriately (and teach other students that same response pattern). You may have to do this multiple times before it becomes part of the students' repertoire.

Again, sensory input as a function is a bit more complicated, as the response is automatic: Have itch, scratch, and itch disappears or is temporarily relieved. But we can provide items that make it difficult to engage in some of those automatic behaviors.

For students who have difficulty keeping their hands to themselves while walking in the hallway or during in-class transitions, they can hold onto an important envelope or keep their hands in their sleeves. At their desk, students can place their hands onto construction paper cut-outs of hands taped to the top of their desk.

Remember to provide verbal encouragement when you see students using the appropriate behavior, such as "great job keeping your hands on top of your desk!" Older students can have silent earbuds in their ears if noise is overwhelming in certain circumstances (just be sure to check with your administrator for approval if use of technology is a rule violation).

On the opposite end, students can listen to quiet music if sensory input is needed. Music that is near sixty beats per minute is the equivalent of the resting heartbeat. You can search YouTube and other music venues for music that is sixty beats per minute. Classrooms can also use "mood lighting" with soft lamps instead of fluorescent bulbs to cut back on both the visual and sound stimulation that they produce. Be sure to check with your administrator if the lamps are fire-marshal approved.

CHAPTER SUMMARY

In this chapter you learned about the four basic functions of behavior; attention, escape/avoidance, tangible, and sensory input. You read multiple classroom-based examples and scenarios of how these functions play out in the classroom and what your response can be. It is important to remember that, as the teacher, your response to the behavior either increases or decreases the likelihood of the behavior occurring again in the future. You also learned about replacement behaviors. Replacement behaviors will provide the same outcome and meet the same functions as inappropriate behaviors, but they will be socially and age appropriate. In the next chapter you will learn more about how the response to the behavior, or consequence, can influence the behavior and your overall classroom management practices.

REFLECTION QUESTIONS

Q1. In Melissa's scenario, do we need to make changes to her home life in order to impact her overall quality of life, or will our responses in the classroom make a difference? If so, how?

Q2. If we identify the function of a behavior and a significant life event occurs in a student's life, will the function change or is it "permanent"? If so, in what ways?

Q3. Think of the common intervention strategies that you currently use in the classroom. Take a moment to align the intervention into the four function categories (attention, escape/avoidance, tangible, and sensory input). Will you utilize those intervention strategies differently now? If so, how?

Q4. If you notice that a colleague is using a strategy that may not be functionally related to the challenging behavior, how will you help that colleague to understand the function of the behavior and identify a replacement behavior?

Chapter Four

Myths about Consequences

WHAT HAPPENS AFTER

One of the biggest myths in education is that consequences are effective. The first thing that is important to understand is that in behavioral theory, a consequence is what occurs after the target behavior, typically within thirty seconds. Consequences can be positive or negative. You have to take the connotation away from the word. The consequence is merely the result or outcome of the behavior.

What most people are attempting to do is punish or eliminate the behavior. The process of punishment implies that the behavior will be less likely to occur in the future. A "punisher" can be positive (adding something to the environment) or negative (removing something from the environment). An example of a positive punisher would be the addition of a loud noise or pain from touching something hot. An example of a negative punisher would be removing recess or taking away a toy (see table 4.1). The only way to know if it is a punisher is if the behavior occurs less often or does not repeat in the future.

Table 4.1. Description of Positive and Negative Reinforcement and Punishment

	Positive +	Negative −
Reinforcement	Adding something to the environment to *increase* the likelihood of the behavior	Removing something from the environment to *increase* the likelihood of the behavior
Punishment	Adding something to the environment to *decrease* the likelihood of the behavior	Removing something from the environment to *decrease* the likelihood of the behavior

The concern is that often teachers attempt to use "punishers" that do not decrease the occurrence of the behavior. In fact, in many cases the behavior occurs more often. If that is true, the behavior is being reinforced rather than punished. The best or most common example of this is the use of time out or exclusionary practices.

TIME IN OR TIME OUT:
THE OVERUSE OF EXCLUSIONARY PRACTICES

What practitioners and researchers have learned about the use of exclusionary practices such as time out or removal from class is that they are not effective in decreasing challenging behavior. Exclusionary practices can be detrimental to student engagement and can limit access to necessary instructional opportunities. Removal from school via suspensions from school is more often given to students who are already below grade levels, have special needs, or represent subgroups of students who experience disproportionate discipline.

The use of exclusionary practices has been linked to the process termed "the school to prison pipeline." This process is one in which students who experience the overuse of removal from school are also those who are more likely to drop out of school, be involved in the juvenile and potentially adult criminal justice system, and require agency supports such as mental health, medical, and substance abuse supports, and the use of entitlement programs. The students who experience removal from class from time out procedures, office referrals, and suspensions are also most often the students who already struggle to engage and enjoy the educational process. They may come from families and communities who experienced struggles in school—generational disengagement.

Can time out or time away work? Yes. The use of time out can be very effective if used meaningfully. Consider this: In the game of hockey, there is a process of penalties. Those penalties result in a player temporarily being removed from the ice and having to watch the game played without the removed player's involvement or assistance. Such a player really wants to be on the ice, sticking slap shots, attempting goals, and scoring points for the team.

Now consider the student who experiences academic challenges or deficits in writing or math. Engaging in writing or math is not enjoyable. The student is not itching to start that worksheet or draft a paragraph. Time out or time away only works if the child is removed from something she or he wants to be involved in.

Use time out or time away in moderation. Pay attention to whether the behavior decreases or is eliminated after the use of a time out procedure. Utilize time out only when you are confident that the student wants to be engaged in the activity. Examples of how to use time out effectively will be provided later in this chapter. But whenever the behavior does not decrease or if it increases, consider a different strategy.

WHEN CAN TIME OUT WORK IN THE CLASSROOM?

Before describing a number of alternative strategies to use in lieu of exclusionary practices, it is helpful to understand the different kinds of time out and how they may be applied more effectively and strategically. There are two common types of time out procedures. The first is exclusionary; the second is non-exclusionary. Both can be effective if used appropriately.

Exclusionary time out procedures are what the phrase implies. The student is temporarily removed from the environment. The use of exclusionary time out may be done by sending the student to the back of the class, to another teacher's classroom, the office, or out of school. The removal should consist of a predetermined amount of time. A common practice is that a time out should not exceed in minutes the age of the student in years. So if the student is six, the time out should not exceed six minutes. A key to consider is that the use of any punishment procedure should be based on the needs of the student and not based solely on the convenience of the staff member.

Non-exclusionary time out is a bit more complex. The concept is the same. It is a process of removing something pleasurable or preferred temporarily in an effort to decrease the challenging behavior. Essentially the student remains in the classroom but is removed from some aspect of the activity that is occurring. A non-exclusionary time out may be as simple as planned ignoring, which will be described in greater detail in chapter 5. The student may be asked to sit in the back of the room and watch the activity. Think of the hockey penalty box. If a student is not following directions on the playground or in the hallways during passing, he or she may be required to sit passively and watch the other students engage in the activity.

Non-exclusionary time out may also consist of temporarily removing the reinforcer for that student. A full description of a token economy is provided in chapter 8. In a token economy, symbolic money or points are used to signal appropriate behavior. Non-exclusionary time out may include reminding the student that while engaged in challenging behavior, she or he cannot earn points, tickets, tokens, or the like.

It is important to note that students are not able to earn items during the pre-determined non-exclusionary time out, but items are not removed from them. If you were to remove or take away an item such as points, tickets, or stickers that have been previously earned, you might instigate a power struggle and imply that you are responsible for the outcomes of the behavior. This can be done by stating, "You are not currently earning your points. When I see that you are sitting appropriately, you will be earning your points again." By letting the children know that their own behavior prevents them from earning a reward, they are able to connect their behavior with the outcome. This is an important step toward self-awareness.

ALTERNATIVES TO EXCLUSIONARY PRACTICES

There are hundreds of other strategies that can be used instead of time out or time away, especially if you are finding that exclusionary practices aren't working. The first thing to explore is functional or logical consequences. As the name implies, this is a process of matching the function of the behavior to the logical result of the behavior.

An example of a logical outcome or consequence is when a student who tips over a desk, knocks papers off the table, or tears down items on a bulletin board is made to clean the mess up. A student who hurts someone's feelings is required to apologize to that person or write a letter of apology. A student who runs in the hallway would be asked to go back to the beginning point and walk. A student who performs that logical consequence should then be verbally praised for engaging in the appropriate behavior.

In other examples of functional outcomes, a student who is attention-seeking would be actively ignored or a student who is attempting to escape or avoid would have to complete the task. Some of these functional consequences may also be natural or occur in the natural environment. A child who tips his chair back may tip too far and fall. A child who runs in the hallway may slip. A child who yells in class may be rejected by his peers.

There are also numerous strategies that can be used to deter future misbehavior or to teach appropriate behavior. Some readers may feel that without the traditional "punishers" students will run amuck. Again, the science of behavior has shown that if the behavior continues to occur, it is being reinforced. Ask yourself if, each time a "consequence" is provided, the behavior has decreased or stopped. A more holistic and effective strategy is to align the consequence to the behavior and focus on teaching the behaviors that we want to see.

Descriptions of some of the strategies listed below (table 4.2) are included in future chapters.

Table 4.2. Possible Alternatives to Exclusionary Practices

Possible Alternatives to Exclusionary Practices	
1. Activity/Privilege loss	26. Parent conference
2. Administration check-ins	27. Parent supervision
3. After-school detention	28. Peer mediation
4. Behavior agreement	29. Phone call to parents
5. Behavioral self-monitoring	30. Positive behavioral supports/Multitiered systems of support
6. Campus beautification	31. Precise requests
7. Check In/Check Out behavior education program	32. Premack Principle
8. Classroom consequence hierarchy	33. Problem-solving process with student
9. Community service	34. Redirection/Reminder/Prompting
10. Conflict resolution	35. Referral for school-based evaluation/In-school staffing
11. Cool off/Break pass	36. Referral to building-based support staff
12. Corrective feedback	37. Referral/Recommendation to outside counseling agency/Diversion program
13. Daily home note	38. Reflection activity
14. Early intervention strategies	39. Restitution
15. Errorless learning	40. Restorative Justice/Practices
16. Family/Caregiver involvement	41. Reteach behavioral expectations
17. In-class detention/In-class suspension	42. Role-play activity
18. In-school suspension	43. Saturday school
19. Individual/Small-group counseling	44. Schedule change/Alternate schedule
20. Letter of apology	45. Service learning
21. Level/Point system	46. Social skills training
22. Limiting social time	47. Structured behavior intervention plan
23. Lunch detention	48. Time out/Time away
24. Mini-course/Skill module	49. Violence prevention program
25. Overcorrection/Repeated practice	50. Youth court/Mock trial

PREVENTION IS THE BEST MEDICINE

Can punishers be effective in the classroom? Yes, they can. They need to be done intentionally, strategically, and with compassion and awareness. However, the best practice is to avoid the need for the use of punishers or exclusionary practices.

The following fable best depicts the importance of prevention:

> Three men were spending the day relaxing by a riverside. As they ate their lunch, one man noticed a child in the river. The men assumed the child was playing and swimming in the river, and they continued to attend to their lunch. Soon after, another child was seen floating in the river. The men suddenly realized the children in the river were not playing. They were in fact struggling to stay above water.
>
> Before long, the river was full of small children struggling to swim. The three men jumped up, fearing for the lives of the children and hopeful that they could save them. Two of the men quickly ran toward the riverbank and began devising a plan. The third man began running upstream. The other two men, eager to jump in and pull the children out, were confused by his actions. They wondered why he would be running away from where the children could be seen drowning. The third man continued to run upstream, determined *to find the place where the children were and stop them from falling into the river.*

As an educator, you often have to react to the circumstances. You have to put out the fires, save the "drowning" children, and respond to the crisis or concern of the moment. And that will always be needed. However, there are many instances in which, with the right strategies, plans, procedures, and techniques, you can prevent the crisis from occurring. We could proverbially prevent the children from falling into the river. Ask yourself: What would you rather spend your time addressing?

Prevention is difficult. It requires that you heavily invest in a process on the front end. It necessitates spending more time and effort to plan, organize, and schedule. But if you consider the amount of time consumed by addressing challenging behavior, the time spent on planning to avoid disruptive, challenging, or aggressive behavior becomes well spent.

CHAPTER SUMMARY

The consequence of a behavior is what occurs immediately after the behavior. Often you are not responsible for delivering the consequence; the natural environment does so. But when you can affect an outcome, you must do so if an undesirable behavior continues to occur. You can do it by strategically setting up punishment procedures that intentionally address the challenging behavior and effectively work to decrease it.

The procedures may be exclusionary, however, the most effective process is to establish an environment of prevention. If the environment is predictable, safe, engaging, and differentiated, it is less likely that you will experience difficult behavior and have to rely on consequence procedures. On the occasion that consequence procedures have to be used, ensure that they relate to the behavior, teach appropriate behavior, and focus on the needs of the student.

REFLECTION QUESTIONS

Q1. How much time, on average, do you feel you spend addressing challenging or disruptive behavior (reprimanding or correcting behavior, writing referrals, reteaching expectations, etc.)? How much time would you be willing to invest in changing routines, procedures, and processes to be more preventative?

Q2. Pick two of the alternatives to suspension and apply them to a situation in the classroom. How did they work?

Q3. If you utilize a process of time out and a student continues to engage in the challenging behavior, how can you adapt the process so that it is more effective?

Q4. What are strategies that you have used to decrease challenging behavior? Why do you believe they worked? How can you apply those strategies to other situations?

Chapter Five

Opposites Attract

*Interventions Aligned
to Challenging Behavior*

This chapter is going to walk you through several common challenging behaviors, the matching desired behaviors, and several strategies to use to address the behaviors. The idea is that for most challenging or disruptive behaviors, there are easy-to-implement techniques to decrease the behaviors. There is nothing magical here; these are merely suggestions to add to your toolbox—approaches to take that may help you in the classroom and assist students in being more successful.

DEFIANCE

- Challenging Behavior: Defiance (resistance, opposition, lack of obedience)
- Desired Behavior: Accepting Responsibility

Intervention 1: Verbal De-Escalation

Verbal de-escalation is a process of identifying stages of challenging behavior and meeting the needs of the student in that stage. Verbal de-escalation requires that the adult remain calm and in control. This can be accomplished by using a relaxed volume and tone of voice. De-escalation techniques are best used when a student is still rational and has not lost control.

You want to provide relevant and realistic answers to questions that the student may have. If a student asks why he or she needs to do math, it is better to respond with a straightforward answer such as, "this is the time of day when math is scheduled," as opposed to a lecture about the importance of math for future employment. Children live in the moment and desire responses that address their immediate needs.

A student who challenges you is likely attempting to drag you into a power struggle. A challenging student is most likely working to gain control of a situation or environment. Ignore the challenge but not the student.[1] Do not reprimand or give directives about the challenging behavior; instead focus on the needs of the student. This can be done by setting limits that are clear and enforceable, while reminding such students to use coping strategies such as taking deep breaths, removing themselves to a calming area, utilizing sensory tools, or counting to five. This can also be accomplished by briefly addressing the student's concern in one to two sentences: Be clear, refrain from using any jargon, provide single-step directions, and then walk away. It is harder to pick up the rope on the other end of a power struggle if you are not close enough to continue to be engaged in the argument.

Intervention 2: Redirection

Redirecting the behavior is the process of placing the focus away from the challenging behavior and toward something or somewhere more productive. Redirecting the behavior quickly often allows the brain to reset, to readjust and refocus on more appropriate behaviors. Redirecting can be as simple as changing the focus of the conversation to more complex procedures.

Distracting for cooperation consists of briefly completing a more-preferred task or topic as a bridge to the less-desired activity. If a student has to engage in a complex math sequence and is becoming frustrated, you could discuss a topic that you know the student is interested in, for example, motorcycles. In the process of the conversation direct the topic back to the task. How many pounds is a cruising motorcycle compared to a dirt motorcycle? What would that convert to in kilograms? How much faster does the dirt bike go compared to the heavier street bike?

Accepting an alternative behavior requires that you allow the student to engage in the behavior but in a more appropriate manner. For instance, if a student is coloring or writing on the desk, give him or her a piece of paper to continue. It may not be the ideal behavior, but by allowing a student some brief time to engage in a preferred activity, she or he may be more apt to join the classroom activity. To students who are calling out answers in an attempt to always be first, provide a stack of sticky notes and a timer to gauge how quickly they can write their responses. This may address their want to be competitive and correct.

An antiseptic bounce is when you provide the child a temporary activity that is in another location. This can be an errand to another teacher's classroom or the front office. You can put a small note in an envelope and have the child deliver it to someone. The student could be asked to staple important papers together or collect and dispose of the recycling. You can create a "Top Secret" mission that the student has to perform.

It is important to do any of these activities at the *first sign* of defiant behavior. You want to be attuned to the triggers or precursor behaviors that signal that challenging behavior is likely. By waiting too long or until the behavior is directly challenging, you may be inadvertently reinforcing it by providing escape from non-preferred tasks or activities. If you catch the defiance in the beginning and redirect it, you can avoid more significant and disobedient behaviors.

NONCOMPLIANCE

- Challenging Behavior: Noncompliance (engaging in behaviors other than those instructed)
- Desired Behavior: Following Directions

Intervention 1: Behavioral Momentum

Behavioral momentum[2] is a strategy derived from applied behavior analysis. The idea follows the same logic as physical momentum. An object in motion will stay in motion. In behavioral momentum you rely on the same resistance to change of physical momentum but also include matching rates of reinforcement.

With behavioral momentum you want to begin with a series of behaviors that are likely to be completed and include frequent reinforcement for engaging in those behaviors. You then gradually increase the demand toward the less-preferred behaviors. In technical terms, you use high probability demands (things the student already likes doing) prior to using a low probability demand (things the student likes less or does not like at all).

A classroom example of behavioral momentum is to request small, simple tasks to be completed. It is best to use three high probability requests before the lower probability request. For younger students you can even use a Simon Says approach ("touch your nose," "touch your ears," "touch your forehead," "open your book"), being sure to include verbal or tangible praise when each task is completed. For some students, just by virtue of making things more playful, you can encourage more compliance toward non-preferred activities, like opening a book and beginning to read.

You can also use a natural progression of tasks in order to build behavioral momentum. An example may look like the following:

1. "Please help me hand out these papers."
2. "Great job handing out papers. Thank you."
3. "Now please help me straighten out the desks."

4. "You are very good at straightening desks. Good work."
5. "Please erase the work on the board."
6. "Wow! The board is so clean."
7. "Thank you for all of the help. Now you have a clean space on the board to begin your work."
8. "Please do the first two problems from the worksheet on the board."

Notice that each higher probability request was made as a statement as opposed to a question. Also notice that each behavior was followed with specific praise for compliance. Once the student is fairly proficient with the higher probability tasks and engaging in the lower probability task, you can consider decreasing the number of higher probability requests.

Remember to picture in your mind how physical momentum works. A ball is already round, so it will roll easily. The high probability tasks need to be easy for the student to engage in. You need to start that ball rolling down the hill so that it picks up speed. Be specific with your initial requests. The hill has to be long enough to build up speed. Use at least three high probability requests initially. The hill doesn't have a wall at the bottom. Work in the lower probability task so that it doesn't stop the ball from rolling but helps to keep moving it along.

Intervention 2: Precise Requesting

Being precise in your requests[3] is a technique to help increase consistency in how requests are made. Consistency is one of the essential components to creating happy and healthy classrooms. For students who thrive on consistency, using precise requests can assist in creating a consistent and safe classroom environment. Being precise means that you use simple, brief directions. This can also help you as a teacher build healthy relationships with students.

Before using precise-requesting procedures, you'll need to have a solid consequence or outcome hierarchy as described in chapter 2. Precise requests rely on using a pattern to make requests and using the same pattern to respond. It is important to be prepared for the student to either follow through or not follow through with the task.

To use a process of precise requests, first start by using a "please" request: "Please open your reading book and begin with the first chapter." Allow five to ten seconds of wait time to allow the student to process and follow through with the request. If the student begins the task, provide specific praise. If the student does not begin the task, you use the next step in the process.

After a please statement and wait time has been used, you may need to use a "need to" statement (e.g., "you need to open your reading book and begin the first chapter"). Again, allow wait time. If the student begins the task, provide specific praise. If the student does not begin the task, inform the student of the first step in your consequence hierarchy. This is typically a verbal warning.

You can begin the process again from the "please" request after taking that first step on the consequence hierarchy. You won't want to repeat the process more than three times for the same request. You will think you sound like a broken record, but that is what makes the procedure effective. It is most effective when the student is aware of the items on the consequence hierarchy, because the student may be discouraged by harsher outcomes for not complying. Just as important is providing verbal or tangible praise when the student does comply with the request.

LACK OF MOTIVATION

- Challenging Behavior: Lack of Motivation (struggling with goal orientation, and task initiation and completion)
- Desired Behavior: Intrinsic Motivation

Intervention 1: Do This, Not That

There are several strategies that can be used in a "do this, not that" technique. The simplest way to increase motivation is to use topics, activities, and tasks that are aligned to students' interests, skills, and strengths. Another common strategy is to reduce the length or difficulty of the task by differentiating the lesson based on the students' learning style, ability, interest, and attentiveness.

Along those lines is a technique of strategically reducing assignments so that students are able to "do this, not that." The strategy works by allowing students to complete portions of the work to earn the reduction of the assignment length. For each predetermined number of problems or portions of material that are successfully completed, the student earns the opportunity to choose which portions or problems to skip.

This strategy is best used when material does not have to be learned or practiced sequentially, such as math problems, letters, or isolated sentences. You will need to determine the amount of work that must be completed and the subsequent amount of work that can be skipped. For example, on a math worksheet, students who complete five math problems can choose three to skip. Students given ten sentences to modify can choose four to skip. You'll want to begin with a small ratio that you can increase once you find the student to be more likely to persist in a non-preferred task. You may have to start with a one-to-one ratio initially: one problem completed, one problem skipped.

This technique allows a student who struggles to persist in tasks and lacks motivation the opportunity to control the amount of work and feel less pressure by the volume of work. You want to work up to greater and greater amounts of work being completed at one time. Don't be worried if you have to start small and there is not a great deal of work being completed in each session. If you are able to persist with the technique you should be able to strategically build toward the full task within a few weeks.

Intervention 2: Interest-Boosting

Interest-boosting is aligned to differentiating instruction. When you differentiate your instruction you are planning for a variety of abilities, interests, and skills. When you are boosting interest you are focusing on the topics that you know the student is motivated by or interested in.

To begin the technique, you want to understand what the students are interested in. This can be done through conversation, an interest inventory, or survey. The goal is to show personal interest in the student and align your instruction to what the student in interested in. For instance, does the student like comic books, a specific TV show, motorcycles, sports, clothes, or beauty? Engage the students in a discussion about their topic of interest. When you have a consistent, reciprocal flow of conversation, introduce the non-preferred activity by tying it to the topic of interest.

As in the earlier redirection example, if the student is interested in cars and is required to complete a complex math problem, begin a conversation about cars. Ask what kind of car the student likes. Does he or she have to do repairs on the car? When doing repairs, does she or he have to calculate the correct torque or liquid combination? At that point you may be able to introduce the less-preferred math problem.

The process requires some knowledge of the student's topic of interest but can also be done using a series of questions to learn more about that interest. The hardest part is working in the less-preferred topic. Practice this technique with other staff to become proficient at knowing how to introduce the academic topic into an interest conversation.

NEED FOR CONTROL

- Challenging Behavior: Need for Control (difficulty with schedule changes, unfamiliar routines, new or novel tasks or people)
- Desired Behavior: Acceptance of Options

Intervention 1: First-Then

All humans desire control over their environment. That should not be a privilege saved only for adults. Children also thrive when their environment

Table 5.1.   Examples of First-Then Strategy

First	Then
Complete 5 math problems.	Take a 5-minute break.
Write 2 paragraphs on desert animals.	Earn a sticker for your sticker chart.

is predictable, transparent, and safe. In all possible circumstances, it is important to maintain the procedures and routines that have been established for the classroom and be consistent in applying rewards for appropriate behavior and outcomes to challenging behavior.

An additional strategy that can be used to help students feel in control is based on the aforementioned Premack Principle.[4] The Premack Principle, or Grandma's Law, occurs when a high probability (highly preferred) activity serves as a reinforcer for a low probability (less-preferred) activity. In other words, as Grandma would state it, "you can eat your dessert after you eat your vegetables."

The principle can be applied by using the phrase first-then or when-then (see table 5.1). The principle can also be applied either visually, using a first-then board, or verbally, using the words first-then to explain the routine to the student: "First write two sentences; then you can take a two-minute break"; or "first clean your area; then you can join the group activity."

Intervention 2: Preferential Seating

A commonly underutilized technique is strategically adjusting where a student is seated. Teachers are amazing at making seating charts, rearranging groupings, and identifying needs based on the lesson or assignment. One area that may be forgotten is where a student is seated based on social or emotional needs.

Is the student seated in an area where there is significant distraction such as near a window, door, or high traffic area? Is the student seated in an area that is safe, with a view of the door, a quick "escape" route, a calming atmosphere? Is the student seated so there will be minimal transition? Can you quickly scan the room and see the student from all angles? These may be additional questions to consider when designing the seating charts. They may be especially important for a student who is struggling with control, based on a history of trauma or traumatic events.

When considering seating arrangements, ask where they feel they will be most productive and comfortable. Converse about pros and cons. Consider offering choices for seating based on specific tasks to minimize distraction or encourage calm and safety. Create a zone or area in the class that the student can go to remove himself or herself from something that is overstimulating. A safe zone or calming area could be a small corner of the room that has comfortable items, a timer (to encourage returning to the instructional environment), relaxing music, and the like.

Intervention 3: Equal Choices

Offering a choice in seating is one strategy to assist with control issues. Another example of providing strategic control is providing equal choices. It allows the teacher some control over what can be offered and the student a sense of control by being able to pick between items. It is really a win-win.

Equal choices can be as simple as having a student pick between the red chair or the blue chair, the pencil or the pen, a seat at the circle rug or at a desk. Equal choices can also be working out the math problem on the whiteboard in the front of the classroom or at the student's desk, or allowing the student to start a worksheet at the top or the bottom.

If this strategy is applied effectively and consistently, it can allow students to feel they have some opportunity to be in control of the decisions that are made. Many students who struggle with control are often seeking their voice, their ability to have a say in what happens around them. Especially those students who have experienced challenges in life or trauma are making every effort to gain back a sense of control and power that has been removed from them. The often quick and easily implemented strategies described above help students to gain back that sense of control and belonging.

DISRUPTION

- Challenging Behavior: Class Disruption (calling out, being verbal at inappropriate times, excessive joking or talking)
- Desired Behavior: Working Quietly/Raising Hand

Intervention 1: Planned Ignoring

An old adage is that it is best to water the roses and ignore the weeds. In behavioral terms, you want to attend to the things that you want to see and ignore some of the behaviors that you don't want to see. An important caveat is that it is necessary to attend to behaviors that pose a safety risk. If there is imminent danger or a safety concern, follow the classroom procedures and consequence hierarchy or the crisis/safety plan that has been established.

But you can ignore minor behaviors, such as calling out, talking excessively, and class clowning. This works when the behavior is identified as attention-seeking behavior. This also works when you have a consistent strategy in place and all staff are implementing the plan across settings. It may even be necessary to teach the other students in the class when and how to ignore some behaviors.

To implement planned ignoring, begin by knowing and understanding the target behaviors and function of the behavior. Do the adults or the peers in the classroom primarily maintain the behavior? Does the behavior ever escalate to a safety risk so that planned ignoring may not be effective? Will all staff be willing and able to ignore the minor behaviors? With that information in hand, a plan can be developed that will pinpoint what behaviors should be ignored, by whom, when, and where. This plan should be communicated with the student. Remind students that when they are following the classroom rules and expectations, they are working toward earning their reward.

Be prepared for what is called an extinction burst. Know in advance that the behavior will likely get worse before it gets better. This occurs because the student has grown accustomed to getting a reaction from the adults or peers. A student who no longer gets that reaction may try harder, longer, or in more unique ways to get that attention. Be consistent, be persistent, and be prepared. If the strategy is applied effectively, you will water the beautiful roses and have a lovely garden of good behavior.

Intervention 2: Pivot Praise

The use of praise in general is more consistently applied at the elementary school level than the secondary level; however, praise is an effective tool to use with all age groups, children and adults. Praise in general should be specific, consistent, and aligned to the classroom rules or school expectations. For example, "I like the way that Cesar has his materials ready, is facing the teacher, and is following our class rule of being ready to learn." It is important to determine if you are praising effort, ability, or performance, to ensure the praise is meaningful to the student.

Pivot praise works on the theory of positive peer pressure. That being said it will be most effective with students who revere their teacher and peers' approval. Pivot praise works by reinforcing the appropriate behavior of the students in the class to encourage other students to engage in the same behavior.

To use pivot praise, simply identify the students in the class who have followed the directive and provide specific praise aloud to those students:

- "I like the way that Gene is sitting."
- "I like how Lilliana is sitting at her desk with her materials ready."
- "I like that Tyrese is seated now."

The intent is that students will hear the positive praise being provided to the other students and want that same praise once they have followed the direction.

Intervention 3: Behavioral Agreement/Contract

The challenging behavior that a student is exhibiting to gain control may be so intense or occur so frequently that a more formal agreement between the student and the teacher needs to be created. Creating a behavioral agreement or contract can accomplish this. The agreement should be a goal for the student to work toward that the student is willing to work toward.

One component of a behavioral agreement should include the desired behavior. The student has likely heard plenty of times what challenging behavior is. The agreement should focus the attention toward the desired behavior.

The agreement should also have an attainable goal and time frame. The goal can always be adjusted as needed, but consider that it should be something the student can accomplish in two to three weeks. The goal should be aimed at increasing the desired behavior (the undesired behavior should naturally decrease with replacement of the desired behavior).

In addition, the agreement should have what the student is working toward. What will the student earn at the end of the agreed-upon time frame for following the parameters of the agreement? The agreement should also contain the specific conditions to earn that reward, and it can include any consequences for not following the agreement.

Both the teacher and the student review the agreement and sign it. The family can also be included and sign the agreement. A sample agreement is below, in figure 5.1.

Behavior Agreement	
My behavior goal:	Complete all work prior to the end of the period
When I intend to reach my goal:	4 weeks
The reward I'm working toward:	Pick two assignments to skip
What I need to do every day to reach my goal and reward:	Organize my time with my calendar app, focus on the teacher, ignore students talking to me, ask for help, and cover chunks of the work so I don't get overwhelmed
Teacher Signature:	
Student Signature:	
Parent Signature:	

Figure 5.1.   Example of Elements for a Behavior Agreement

IMPULSIVITY

- Challenging Behavior: Impulsivity (fidgeting, being easily distracted, difficulty following directions in a timely manner)
- Desired Behavior: Think First/Wait

Intervention 1: Proximity Control

Impulsivity may have a number of causes. No matter if the cause is medical or hormonal or developmental, there are techniques that can be used to support students who have difficulty with impulsive behaviors. There may be a medical component to a child's impulsivity, but it is also true that impulsive behavior is also developmentally appropriate at certain stages of adolescence. Understanding the root causes of impulsive behavior can be helpful, but it is not necessary when developing interventions to help students be successful.

A quick and easy intervention is proximity control. The saying "when the cat is away, the mice will play" is precisely what can ring true if a teacher is not utilizing proximity. Proximity control means moving closer to students in need of encouragement for appropriate behavior. In order to monitor behavior, address challenging behavior, and provide corrections and rewards, you need to be near the student.

One technique for proximity is using a process of random-patterned movement in the classroom. This process will assist in determining student behavior and engagement with the lesson. Random patterns will also create the opportunity to monitor triggers of challenging behavior, allow for easy access to assist students in need, and provide the ability to quickly praise and reward appropriate behaviors.

When using proximity control be sure that you are close enough to the student to provide support but not so close that you are invading privacy or personal space. If you are using a random pattern, you will likely discourage students from being off task or off topic. If you are strategically placing yourself by a student who is experiencing challenging behavior, be sure you are not providing too much attention to inappropriate behavior. It may be necessary to combine planned ignoring with proximity control in some cases.

Intervention 2: Shaping

Impulsivity is correlated to the ability to wait for a preferred item, activity, or person. A tool to increase students' ability to wait is derived from the behavioral principle of shaping behavior. Shaping involves the reinforcement of successive approximations toward a desired behavior. In the case of shaping wait time, it is a process of teaching a student to anticipate and tolerate longer periods of time before a reinforcer is delivered.

To begin the process, the desired wait time and appropriate behavior should be determined. In most cases the wait time should be determined based on the intensity and frequency of the behavior. A student should not be expected to wait for a week to receive the preferred item or activity. Consider what is developmentally appropriate and what is typical of most students in the class.

Once the chosen wait time has been established it is necessary to plan for what the approximations will be. If the desired wait time is ten minutes, consider increments of two minutes. Begin the process by immediately providing the desired item/activity. This will need to be done several times or over several periods of time or days. For example, if the student requests the item, provide it to him or her immediately. Once the student is fluent in asking for the desired item appropriately then you can begin lengthening the time between deliveries. That time may need to be shorter in the beginning, a few seconds, and then extended to minutes. This timing will be dependent on the behavior and the student. If the student engages in challenging behavior after an extended period of time, shorten the time again for several trials.

Another strategy to shape wait time is to begin by placing the item on the student's desk. Gradually, with successive approximations, the item would be moved farther and farther away to create both visual and temporal distance. This is best for students who learn with visual modality or who struggle with abstract concepts.

OFF-TASK BEHAVIOR

- Challenging Behavior: Off-Task Behavior (attending to other work/activity that is not relevant to the instructed task/activity)
- Desired Behavior: On-Task Behavior

Intervention 1: Chart Game

The chart game[5] process turns learning appropriate behavior into a game. Students have a visual game board that they are earning moves on, in order to win a reward at the end. This is a great strategy for students who like competition and games.

An easy way to create the game boards is to download connect-the-dot pictures from the Internet and print them out. Each time the student engages in a predetermined appropriate behavior, he or she earns the opportunity to connect one dot to the next. Once students have completed the connect-the-dots image, they earn the reward they have been working toward.

Another easy example is an image that has sections that can be colored in, such as a snake with different segments or a thermometer that students can color until it is fully colored in. The difficulty, complexity, and number of segments (or dots) should be determined based on the challenging behavior and the student's ability. A good rule is that the frequency of connecting a dot or coloring a segment should closely align to how often the student engages in the challenging behavior. For example, a student who calls out every five minutes in a thirty-minute period should have an image with approximately five to six dots or segments to color in. The complexity can also be increased based on the student's age or grade level. At the secondary level the dots can be for sections of work or complete assignments. It would still make sense to have the student start small and work up to larger chunks of work.

Intervention 2: Token Economy

One of the most common behavioral strategies employed in classrooms is the token economy. Token economies work on a premise similar to the chart game and the technique of shaping. The desired behavior is reinforced with symbolic items that can be turned in for a larger or more-preferred item, much the way money is turned in for preferred items such as shoes or nice dinners after a paycheck is earned.

The most common example for understanding the token economy comes from dolphin training. Anyone that has been to an aquarium and watched a training show has seen token economies at work. The trainer begins by pairing the dolphins' favorite food, fish, with a sound, typically a whistle. Eventually the dolphin learns that the sound equals food. The trainer can then use the sound more frequently and periodically give the dolphin a fish.

In the classroom, it is often much easier. Determine what will be used as the symbolic whistle. Most token economies use fake money or tokens. Stickers and points can also be used, but since most students already understand money, it is an easy place to begin. Different denominations and images can be found online to download and print.

Create a school store or list of items that can be purchased with the money once it has been earned and establish how often or when money can be turned in. For example, a catalog of items could be created that students can view on Wednesday and purchase on Friday. A school store could be created for students to shop during lunch periods. A treasure box could be available at the end of each day.

When designing your store, be mindful of what items students would want. Would they prefer school supplies or trinkets? It is also important to consider how much items cost compared to what the students are earning. If students can earn up to one hundred dollars a day, the items in the store should be appropriate for someone earning up to $500 in a week. Be prepared to have savers and spenders. Some students will buy a lot of low-priced items and some students will save money to buy one high-priced item. The cost and content of the store will likely need to be adjusted based on use and student interest.

Another common consideration is what to do when students counterfeit money. And they will. First, celebrate—yes, celebrate. This means that they have bought into your token economy and are willing to do something against the rules to get a desired item. Then make adjustments:

- Change the color or image on the money.
- Sign and date the back of the money upon delivery.
- Create a bank where you deposit the money instead of handing it directly to the student.
- Utilize old or donated checkbooks to have students keep track of money earned and money spent.
- Consider purchasing one of the online programs that use the same principles as a token economy.

The best part about a token economy is you can target multiple behaviors across the classroom, meet the needs of a diverse group of students, and implement the process with minimal effort or interruption to the learning environment. It also teaches valuable lessons in earning through economics.

CHAPTER SUMMARY

In this chapter strategies to address challenging behavior were organized based on common classroom concerns. While these strategies are a starting point, it is important to focus on the function of the behavior and interventions that address that function. When designing interventions based on a challenging behavior, always be mindful of the needs of the student. It is important to consider age, developmental needs, abilities, and ease of implementation. The best intervention will fail if it is not done with fidelity or integrity.

REFLECTION QUESTIONS

Q1. Trinity is struggling to focus in class. She is often off-task and frequently calls out during instructional times. Other teachers have suggested that she is impulsive and unable to sit for periods of time. Based on this information, Trinity has multiple challenging behaviors. What strategies from this chapter would you attempt and why?

Q2. Jocelyn has a history of abuse and neglect. After reading her file, you know that she was left alone for extended periods of time as a toddler. Her grandfather physically abused her, and she was malnourished as an infant. You have noticed that she will react to loud noises and become easily frightened throughout the day. You are adjusting your seating arrangements for the second semester. What changes do you make for Jocelyn based on her needs?

Q3. Philipe is new to your high school class. It is clear that he can be defiant and often argues when he is presented with a task or direction. Until now, your current rules, expectations, and classroom management strategies have worked for your class. With Philipe in the class now, other students are also becoming more defiant. What strategy or strategies could you use to assist Philipe and the other students in the class?

Q4. You have been asked by your administrator to assist a colleague who is experiencing student behavior challenges in the classroom. You have been allowed to observe the teacher for one day and then spend one hour providing feedback and strategies to assist him or her. What would you look for when observing? What strategies would you discuss? How could you present all of the strategies described in this chapter to the teacher in a short amount of time?

NOTES

1. Crisis Prevention Institute. crisisprevention.com

2. Mace, C. F., Hock, M. L., J. S. Lalli, B. J. West, P. Belfiore, E. Pinter, and D. K. Brown, "Behavioral Momentum in the Treatment of Noncompliance," *Journal of Applied Behavior Analysis* 21, no. 2 (Summer 1988): 123–41, doi: 10.1901/jaba.1988.21-123.

3. De Martini-Scully, D., M. A. Bray, and T. Kehle, "A Packaged Intervention to Reduce Disruptive Behaviors in General Education Students," *Psychology in the Schools* 37, no. 2 (2000): 149–56.

4. Premack, D., "Reversibility of the Reinforcement Relation," *Science*, New Series 136, no. 3512 (April 20, 1962): 255–57.

5. Jenson, William R., Ginger Rhode, and H. Kenton Reavis, *The Tough Kid Tool Box* (Longmont, CO: Sopris West, 1994).

Chapter Six

Focus on What Is Right

$4 + 2 = 6$
$5 - 2 = 3$
$4 + 3 = 8$
$10 + 2 = 12$

What is the first thing that you notice in the list above? Did you quickly see that $4 + 3 = 8$ is incorrect? Most people do. What most people don't focus on is that the other problems are correct. We tend to focus more on what is wrong as opposed to what is right.

This example was done to better understand the power of positivity. As humans, we are wired to instinctively focus on what is wrong in our environment. In the survival of the fittest, it makes sense. If you see a large predator, run. If you see flames, move. In today's society and in our collaborative and global culture, however, it does not suit us well to focus so much on what is wrong.

Researchers and scientists are beginning to understand positivity in greater detail. When you focus on positivity, you see more positivity. Some call it the nature or law of intent. Some consider it part of metaphysics. Experiments have been done at a molecular level to see the impact of positive mental energy on items and substances, including water and rice.

To test the theory, you can do the rice test. The steps are listed below.

Step 1: Cook plain white rice following the manufacturer's instructions.

Step 2: Place half of the rice into two airtight, sealed containers. Label one of the containers "Positive" and the other one "Negative." Place the containers in a dry, cool location.

Step 3: Each day pick up the container labeled "Positive" and say something positive to it. It is important to believe in the positivity; make the statement genuine. Pick up the container labeled "Negative" and yell at it; be angry and mean.

Step 4: Repeat this each day for one week.

You should start to see a difference between the containers of rice. In most cases the container that is yelled at and receives negative energy will spoil faster. You will often see mold form much faster on that rice than on the rice that you say positive statements to.

Now imagine that rice as yourself or your students. After all, we are all made up of molecular energy and we are susceptible to being influenced by the energy around us. If we focus on what is right, we see more of what is right and vice versa.

One process that you can utilize is called "reframing." Reframing is the action of changing the lens through which you see a situation. It is an active process of honing in on the positive.

Take your fist and make a tight circle that you can look through. Find a small object in the distance and focus your fisted circle toward that item. All of your concentration goes toward that object. If your fist has formed a tight circle, it may be all that you can see through your "lens." Now widen your circle slightly by opening your fist. Other objects should come into focus, giving you a bigger picture of the surroundings and environment. Now remove your hand. You can see the entire setting, the whole picture.

We often focus our attention too tightly on what is wrong. By doing so, it becomes difficult to see the entire picture, the setting, the circumstances. By reframing and opening your lens to all of the factors that may impact a student, such as academic deficits, trauma, self-esteem, fear, pressure, anxiety, and so on, as well as strengths, skills, talents, hopes, wishes, and dreams, you are better able to fully address any concerns or challenges. Reframing allows you to view the whole child. Reframing can also do the opposite by closing your lens to see only the good in a student.

BEHAVIOR IS COMMUNICATION

What you say and how you communicate is a large part of the work in education. You likely spend a large part of your day communicating with others, speaking to your students, talking with colleagues. The process of learning and growing requires children to expand their communicative repertoires. Communication is key.

Communication is also a behavior. And behavior is communication. When working to understand a person's behavior it is critical to recognize that he or she may be attempting to communicate something that she or he does not yet have the skills to communicate appropriately.

In chapter 3 you were introduced to the world of functional behavior. In chapter 5 you explored a number of interventions to address specific challenging behaviors. Now you are going to confront the concept that challenging behavior occurs as a means of communicating. The challenging behavior is often a maladaptive way of requesting something that a person is unable to express through words.

Imagine yourself in a foreign country, unable to speak or understand the language. While there may be some requests you can make using body language, there are many nuances that you would miss. For example, you could move your hands toward your mouth as if using eating utensils and likely receive information about food or where to eat. But you probably won't be able to convey to the other person that you are lactose intolerant and can't have any dairy. You can probably use your hands to ask where a bathroom is, but you may not be able to ask for a family restroom with a baby-changing table.

This process of working so diligently to express your needs or ask a question would likely get frustrating after a period of time. It may even cause rational adults to lose their temper. Now, imagine having to go through this process every day to meet your basic needs. It would be exhausting.

In the developmental phases of childhood, full maturity is often not reached until the early to late twenties. For the entire school career of most children and adolescents, they are still developing. Along with that development comes the practice of learning how to ask for what is wanted or needed, how to identify feelings and let another person know about internal thoughts or feelings, and how to express likes and dislikes. You may even know adults who still find this challenging.

A child who yells during class may be experiencing pain from a headache or frustration due to a skill deficit. A teenager who leaves class may be dealing with thoughts of depression or the experience of a traumatic event. Kindergartners who stomp their feet on the ground may be scared of the unknown.

When developing plans to address challenging behavior, one step may be to teach the appropriate way to request what is wanted or needed. For many students this begins with identifying internal feelings, both physical and emotional. There are some tools that can be used to help students make a link between what they are feeling and what they may need or want.

One idea is a wheel of emotion. Make a game-board type of spinning wheel using two pieces of paper. Divide it evenly into multiple parts, and label the parts with different emotions (happy, angry, frustrated, embarrassed, thankful, etc.). Prompt students on a regular basis or when you feel they need to be reminded to identify how they feel in that moment. Be sure to have conversation with them about the emotions, why they chose particular emotions, and what it feels like inside their body when they experience those emotions.

To help younger students link the physical with the emotional, create an image of a blank cartoon body. This can be done on a piece of notebook size paper for an individual student or poster paper for an entire classroom. If you notice a student who seems to be frustrated or happy, have the student point to the body chart and explain where he or she feels that emotion. For example, a student who is frustrated may feel a knot in the stomach or a lump in the throat. A student who is happy may feel light-headed or have a rapid heartbeat. You can try this with toddlers through adolescents.

Another strategy is a feeling log. A timer can be set in the class to beep periodically and randomly. When the beep sounds, students can write or draw how they are feeling at that moment. This can also be coupled with a practice of mindfulness, a deliberate practice of stopping throughout the day and recognizing the subtleties in the environment, how you feel, what you notice by sight and sound. Mindfulness helps you to be present in the moment and cognizant of yourself.

Once students are more aware of their feelings and emotions, they can be taught the skill of communicating what they want and need. Students who exhibit challenging behavior for attention need to learn how to appropriately ask for attention. Do they need to learn to ask for help? Do they need to ask for one-on-one time? Do they need to ask peers to participate in a game or activity with them?

A student who is trying to avoid or escape a task needs to learn to request a break or ask for time away from a challenging activity. A student who takes items from another student can learn how to ask to share or for more time with a preferred item. A child who needs to stand up, listen to music, or doodle to help with concentration would benefit from knowing how to ask for that assistance.

BRAIN SCIENCE AND WHAT
WE ARE LEARNING ABOUT POSITIVITY

Once a child has the tool of communication, the challenging behavior is less effective. The communication part of the brain is activated and new neural paths are created. The more developed and active part of the brain is working.

As humans, we essentially have three brains. The oldest part of the brain is located just above the spine and is typically known as the reptilian brain. That part of the brain is responsible for fight or flight, stimulus and response. A newer part of the brain is the mammalian brain, the reward and punishment center of the brain. And, the frontal lobe, the most newly developed part of the brain, is responsible for language, organization, executive functioning skills, and abstract thought.

Scientists continue to learn about the exponential abilities of our brains. Some researchers are investigating how positive thoughts, communication, and actions affect persons and the environment. One of those scientists is Dr. Martin Seligman, who studies the science of positive psychology.[1] While much of the world of psychology has traditionally been concentrated on how the past impacts a person, the field of positive psychology seeks to identify the influence of positivity.

Positivity is most often categorized into concepts of hope, optimism, and happiness. Students today experience symptoms of mental health disorders and experiences of trauma at astounding rates. As a teacher you are likely to find that nearly one in four students in your class has experienced some form of traumatic event.[2] The effects of trauma and mental health can greatly impact student performance and well-being.

An environment in the classroom and in the school that is focused on positivity, hope, optimism, strengths, the ability for growth, and the like can be beneficial for both students and staff. Achieving this may require a concerted effort by staff to build upon optimism and hope. You may need to practice focusing on what is right and believing that all students are able to grow and learn.

INCORPORATING POSITIVE BEHAVIORAL INTERVENTIONS INTO THE CLASSROOM

One of the most effective strategies to incorporating more positivity into the classroom is the use of Positive Behavioral Interventions and Supports (PBIS).[3] PBIS applies behavior analytic principles to classroom and school settings. PBIS also incorporates foundational principles from positive psychology and infuses them into processes to be proactive and preventative.

PBIS has several foundational components, including leadership and staff commitment, data-based decision-making, expectations and rules, recognition processes, lesson and implementation plans, and an evaluation system. PBIS is also a tiered system of support with much of the prevention and proactive work occurring at a school-wide level. At the classroom level, there are some simple strategies that can be incorporated to increase positivity and focus on prevention.

The first step to take, as with any good plan, is to collect data. These data should focus on the ratio of positive to negative/neutral statements in the class. Have a colleague or peer observe your class several times during different subjects or activities. Ask them to monitor the number of times that you say or do something positive (praise a student, compliment someone, give a high five, smile, etc.) and each time you do something negative or neutral (express that an answer is incorrect, give a directive, reprimand or scold a student, etc.). The ideal ratio is four positives to every one negative or neutral statement. The positive statements and behaviors should also be genuine, specific, observable, and focused on progress and effort.

As described in chapter 5, the token economy allows us to focus on what we want to see and to reward appropriate beharior rather than focusing on decreasing challenging behaviors.

Many of the processes and components of PBIS in the classroom were described in earlier chapters:

- In chapter 2 you learned about classroom procedures and rules. When developing or revising these processes, consider how to incorporate a positive framework.
- In chapter 3 the focus was on the functions of behavior. Understanding the functions of challenging behavior will assist in creating classroom-based plans to address the maladaptive behavior and create effective replacement behaviors.
- In chapter 4 the important message of prevention was emphasized.
- In chapter 5 intervention strategies were provided.
- In chapter 7 you will learn about making data-based decisions.

All of these strategies, tips, tools, and ideas are delivered in a way that incorporates PBIS. After all, PBIS should not be something separate or different; rather, it should be a framework for the classroom, the foundation that drives the work you do.

CHAPTER SUMMARY

In this chapter you refocused and recalibrated to focus more on positive events and behaviors that occur in the environment. While it is often not an intuitive action, focusing on positivity can reestablish a more inviting and nurturing classroom. The act of intentionally concentrating on what you want to see and reinforcing appropriate behavior will have an overall positive effect on you and your students.

There are numerous ways to increase positivity in the classroom from more structured strategies such as PBIS to less structured techniques like reframing. As a classroom teacher you can attend to students' strengths and skills, reward appropriate behavior, build positive foundational frameworks for procedures and routines, and embed structures in the classroom that emphasize positivity.

REFLECTION QUESTIONS

Q1. What are three things that you can do tomorrow to be more positive?

Q2. If you intend to build a token economy, what strategies will you utilize to ensure that students can access preferred items in a timely manner and at an effective cost?

Q3. If you have a coworker or colleague who tends to be negative and pessimistic, what strategies could you use to help build optimism and hope?

NOTES

1. "Dr. Martin Seligman," Authentic Happiness, https://www.authentichappiness .sas.upenn.edu

2. ACES Study: Adverse Childhood Experiences, www.cdc.gov/violenceprevention

3. "Positive Behavioral Interventions and Supports," http://www.pbis.org

Chapter Seven

"Data" Is More than a Four-Letter Word

In the world of accountability, *evaluation* and *assessment data* have become more like curse words than parts of a helpful strategy to use in the classroom. Data-based decision-making has become more of a trendy term than a truly useful process for teachers and students. For data to be helpful it is necessary to understand why we collect data and what we can do with it.

Data are facts. Without data, teams and teachers often spend an exorbitant amount of time guessing and second-guessing the best solution to a problem. With so little time to spare in the teaching day, it is vital to have data to help solve problems. *Data* is so much more than just a four-letter word; it is a four-letter solution.

Collecting data allows you to identify patterns in student and staff behavior. Behavior may occur frequently within a short period of time. Behavior may also occur infrequently, making it difficult to determine why it is occurring. Consider a child who becomes anxious and defiant once or twice a month. The behavior may be seldom, but when it does occur the intensity is high: The child can become aggressive. It is only after collecting data across multiple weeks that a teacher may be able to connect, for example, the child's parental visitation schedule during reunification from a foster family with the aggressive behavior.

Data help to communicate information. Legislation for students with disabilities even requires that data be presented so that families can easily interpret it. Graphic displays of data such as graphs and charts help to communicate clearly and easily the extent, frequency, and intensity of behaviors. Data also help to communicate among colleagues how a student may be doing on a given day, the student's progress toward goals, or how often a new behavior or strategy is utilized. Clear communication about behavior will help collaborating professionals consistently implement plans, understand the effects of changes to the plan or environment, and adjust the plan as necessary.

Data-based decisions are more than just good practice in the classroom. Data are also necessary when working with students who have special needs or are in the response-to-intervention process. Data assist in making reasonable and attainable goals for individual education plans, behavior intervention plans, and classroom behavioral agreements. By utilizing classroom and instructional data, you can understand the impact of your teaching—of each planned lesson—on student learning.

Most importantly, data help to build confidence. If you are able to see that the plan that you create, the lesson that you develop, the goals that you set, the strategies that you explore, the environment and culture that you establish have meaning in the classroom, you will be more confident to continue on your positive path. Practical data will assist in enlisting support from colleagues because the data may clearly reflect your need for support; at which times, for which students, where, and when. Data will support your ability to stand by your decisions as a teacher and to learn and grow in the process.

USING A FOUR-STEP PROBLEM-SOLVING PROCESS

Data collection for problem-solving is not a one-man band. Data collection and making data-based decisions require a team process. Multiple people can collect data, and a team should be reviewing those data to help make decisions. This can be especially helpful if data are collected across multiple settings and people. The team can work together to analyze and understand the data.

The team can also utilize a problem-solving process at any point in the process described below, to determine the target behavior, to decide which data collection tool to use, and to identify what the data are saying. The problem-solving process is a tool that teams can use to interpret and analyze the data. Problem-solving can also be used to better understand when to fade or begin weaning a schedule of reinforcement. For example, students are earning reinforcement (stickers) every five minutes that they are in their seat, and the goal was sitting for five minutes within two weeks. The students have met that goal, so the team may determine that for the next two weeks the time should increase to seven minutes. The team may decide to meet again after another two weeks until eventually it is only reinforcing the sitting behavior every fifteen minutes.

Step 1: Identify the problem. Just as was described in earlier chapters it is crucial to determine what that actual problem behavior is. This can be applied on a grander scale to determine school-wide, personal, or global concern, but for the purposes of this book the focus will be on identifying the challenging behavior or the challenging issue. It is all too common that you will want to jump to finding a solution, but elaborate plans are often drafted and resources spent on misinformation or an incorrect identification of the problem. Become a detective. Ask and interview people who know the student or the situation. Look at records and historical information. Work together as a team to clearly define what the hypothesized problem is.

Step 2: Analyze the problem. To analyze the problem, it will be necessary to understand the why. One way to establish the root cause[1] of an issue is to ask why multiple times. Asking why more than three times requires the team to look beyond the surface of whys and create a list of possibilities. The hope is that after several whys the team will be able to determine a root cause of the concern.

If a student is becoming verbally aggressive and our first assumption is that the student is defiant or oppositional, that does not give us much information to create an effective plan. If we ask why again, perhaps the team will uncover that the student has a challenging home life and is often responsible at home for his or her younger siblings. If you ask why again, the team may discover that the student and his or her younger sibling often go without food while the parents are working double shifts in fear of losing their home.

In asking why again the team discovers that during a social work visit to the home the student revealed a fear of losing the home and often hears his or her parents fight over money and who will be responsible for the children, as they would likely have to give them up or split them between family members. The team now can create a plan to help the student feel safe at school, develop coping strategies, and ensure that the student and sibling are fed multiple times a day.

Step 3: Create a plan. The next step is to take all the gathered information and create a plan that will help the student be successful. In most cases it is best to keep the plan simple, in keeping with the old adage that the simple answer is typically the best. Again, all too many times teams create elaborate and extensive plans that are based on information that is inaccurate, not easily implemented, or not based on the function of the behavior. In order to ensure that a plan will be implemented, be sure to have the entire team agree to the plan, know the roles and responsibilities, have a timeline, and prepare for both consistency and flexibility. The plan should be implemented consistently across people and settings. The team should also be prepared to review the plan and make adjustments as necessary based on the data collected.

Step 4: Determine if the plan is effective. Just as academics are progress-monitored, so too should behavior be. In order to know how and if a student is responding to an intervention, data should be collected (i.e., frequency, duration, intensity, etc.) and reviewed on an ongoing basis. The timeline for review should be based on the intensity and severity of the behavior. The more intense or severe, the more frequently it is reviewed.

This same four-step problem-solving process can be used at the class-wide level as well. If you are struggling with a noisy classroom and having difficulty getting students to pay attention during instruction, you can use the four steps to work toward a solution:

- **Step 1.** Identify that the students are noisy during bell-work and lesson plan introduction.
- **Step 2.** After asking several students to assist in determining why and after collecting data for two weeks, conclude that the bell-work and lesson plan opening activities are not engaging for students.
- **Step 3.** Working with several partner teachers in the same grade and reviewing sample lessons on the district website and Internet, make changes to the bell-work and lessons. An interest inventory survey would also better connect lessons to students' pursuits.
- **Step 4.** Take additional data over two weeks and find that noise levels have decreased and students have expressed greater interest in the content. Note that classroom tardies have also decreased and students have been more likely to arrive to class early or on time.

THE FIVE W'S OF DATA

To begin a process of sound and effective data collection, it is necessary to identify the target and impeding or challenging behavior that is going to be measured. There are several points to consider when determining the target behavior. What challenging behavior is interfering most with the student's learning or the learning of others? What positive behaviors are you trying to increase? Is the behavior measurable and observable?

The data collection process is only as good as the behavior being measured. A behavior is considered measurable and observable when it passes the potato test. If a potato can do it, then it is not a behavior. To be measurable and observable, two independent observers should be able to count the same behavior at the same time from different angles in a room. To ensure consistent data collection on a behavior, an operational definition of the behavior can be created.

An operational definition takes a broad definition of a behavior and creates more categorical and specific guidelines. For instance, many teachers use the term *temper tantrum*. *Temper tantrum* is a very broad term that can encompass hundreds of different behaviors. No two temper tantrums look the same. An operational definition is a definition expanded to say that a temper tantrum begins with clenched fists, crossed arms, and tears, and can escalate to include punching, dropping to the floor, high-decibel screaming, profanity, and flailing fists and feet. Would a stranger who saw this definition be able to collect data on the temper tantrum behavior?

It may feel like the challenging behavior occurs "all of the time." The only way to better understand when the behavior truly occurs is to take frequent or constant data for a period of time until a clear pattern is established. Data should be collected often enough to be able to notice trends and make decisions. This will vary based on the severity and frequency of the behavior and the intent of the data collection. If the behavior occurs infrequently—monthly—and is being collected as part of a student's annual educational plan, the data collection may occur less frequently. For a behavior that occurs up to ten times in a minute and is being monitored as part of a behavior plan that is reviewed weekly, the data will likely be collected on an ongoing basis.

Data on the behavior that is being monitored should be collected in any setting in which it occurs. Data on a behavior that occurs across multiple settings but is only collected in the classroom does not provide sufficient information to make good data-based decisions. Collecting data across settings can also help to identify areas at which the behavior is more or less likely to occur. Once it is established where the behavior is most and least likely to occur, the data collection can focus more on those areas. Problem-solving can center on why the behavior is less likely to occur in a setting and how that may be replicated across multiple settings.

- **Who** are the top one or two students with needs in the classroom?
- **What** are the challenging and positive behaviors?
- **When** is the challenging behavior occuring most and least?
- **Where** is the challenging behavior occuring most and least?
- **Why** is the challenging behavior occurring?

Types of Data Collection

Once the operational definition is clear and when and where data should be collected have been established, the next step is creating the system for data collection. The data collection system should be useful to the team that will be using it to make decisions. The data collection system should be relevant to the behavior being measured. The data system should be easy to use for all persons collecting data. In some cases, the student may also be collecting her or his own data. Data collection can be used for an individual or a classroom depending on what the concerns or challenges are.

Type of Data	Description	When to Use	Tools to Use
Event Recording/ Frequency Count/ Tally	Recording the number of times that a behavior occurs	When the behavior occurs frequently, high probability behaviors, behavior has a clear beginning and end	Tally marks, checkmarks, abacus, hand-held frequency counters, smiley faces, tokens, pennies, paperclips
Behavior Examples: calling out, punching, kicking, word recognition, responses, self-injurious behaviors			
Interval Recording	Recording whether a behavior occurs or does not occur during intervals of specified time periods	When an estimate of the number of times a behavior occurs is sufficient, when it is difficult to attend to the occurrence of the behavior during long periods of time	Charts, tables, plus or minus indicators
Behavior Examples: on-task, talking to peers, sitting in seat/in area			
Duration Recording	Recording the length of time a behavior occurs	When the behavior occurs for longer periods of time; behavior has a clear beginning and end	Timer, clock, stopwatch
Behavior Examples: screaming, peer interactions, length of restroom breaks, out of seat, time to complete assignments			
Latency Recording	Recording the amount of time it takes for a student to begin the behavior	When the student is cued/directed to begin a behavior and time lapses until the behavior occurs	Timer, clock, stopwatch
Behavior Examples: beginning an academic task, putting toys away, following the teacher's directions			
Intensity	Recording the level of a behavior	When the behavior can be broken down into	Decibel meter, online decibel/noise meter, teacher created chart
Behavior Examples: difficult task, noise, class/instructional disruption			

Figure 7.1. Types of Classroom Data to Assist with Problem-Solving

With regard to types of data collection tools, the options are endless. Rank-ordered from most to least effective, the data collection methods below are most often used by teachers.

1. Data/behavior sheets and associated graphs or charts (event recording, interval recording, frequency, duration, latency, etc.)

2. Teacher-developed checklists
3. Formal observations
4. Anecdotal records
5. Academic grades/credits
6. Student work/permanent products

This book will focus on the first set of data collection options: the observational recording systems (figure 7.1). They will provide the most accurate and consistent data to problem-solve. Observational recording data is also more objective than the other types of data.

Two additional helpful data collection tools are scatterplot and ABC data. Both help to organize data into clear patterns. Scatterplot and ABC data can be used in congruence with other types of data collection to get multiple perspectives and sources of data to make efficient decisions.

ABC data is important to the functional behavioral assessment process. ABC is an acronym for Antecedent, Behavior, and Consequence. Collecting ABC data is as simple as creating a three-column chart and collecting anecdotal information for each column. For a period of time the teacher can collect information about what happens immediately before (antecedent) and after (consequence) the target or impeding behavior. Collecting ABC data can also help to understand more about the behavior that is being observed. If there is little consistency in the antecedents and consequences, is the target behavior accurate? Clear patterns in the antecedents and consequences should develop quickly in the data collection process.

Scatterplots are another good means of identifying patterns in behavior. A scatterplot is a grid or table broken into specific time periods. The time periods could align to class periods or subjects. When the behavior occurs within a time period that frame of the grid is colored in or tallies are placed in that grid. By doing this, patterns in the grids can be identified. A scatterplot collects and graphs data simultaneously. The scatterplot can be a useful tool to use when determining the most and least likely times a behavior occurs.

ASKING THE RIGHT QUESTIONS: ANALYZING YOUR DATA

There are a number of reasons why it is important to become a data lover. Now that data is no longer a curse word, you have the opportunity to fall in love with what data can do for you. The process of collecting the data can be cumbersome in some cases but the analysis should be liberating.

The team should collect data on both a baseline (data prior to intervention) and ongoing progress-monitoring (data during intervention) basis. Create a spreadsheet and graphs using a graphing program and watch the data come to life. Scatterplots and line, bar, or pie graphs should paint a clear picture of what is happening with the student. Is there improvement? Is the intervention being implemented consistently? Are there times of day or subjects that are more challenging? Are there people who the behavior is more likely to occur around? Are there days of the week that create concerns?

Data can allow the team to understand the effectiveness and efficiency of the interventions that have been put into place. Data help to determine how the student is responding to the intervention. The data can also ensure that the team is working smarter not harder. In more extreme cases data analysis can help a team to determine a student's readiness to reintegrate in more general education opportunities.

The team will need to determine if the student is making progress toward the established goals. For example, a behavior that is typically occurring forty times a week a goal may be to decrease to thirty in a week and then twenty in a week so that in a month it is near zero. You can show that by creating a goal or aim line on the graph. A rule of thumb for determining progress toward a goal of decreasing a challenging behavior is that if four of the last six data points fall below the goal or aim line the student is making progress. This would be vice versa for a behavior that is intended to increase (replacement behavior).

The team can review the data for trends and patterns or the general direction of the behavior change. The team can review and discuss if the behavior is having an impact on the overall quality of life or social significance for the student. The team may need to determine if, based on the data, the intervention is providing more independence, inclusion, access, and ability to communicate needs effectively. If adjustments are required the team can alter the classroom environment, instructional methods, or transitioning process.

The team can also include the parents in the data process. After providing parents with graphs of data showing progress, call or meet with them to discuss what the data have shown. If appropriate, show parents the effects of different instructional strategies and describe how decisions about instructional strategies are made. Ask parents if they are satisfied with the progress that their child has been making on his or her goals and objectives. If satisfied, do they see any changes that could be made to increase progress? If not satisfied, do they have any suggestions about how to increase their child's progress?

CHAPTER SUMMARY

In this chapter the intent and purpose of data collection were described. While data collection can be time-consuming there are strategies that can be used to help streamline the process and help to ensure consistency and accuracy. With good data, good decisions can be made and quick progress toward success can often be seen. Data can be collected and displayed in a number of ways to help in the plan development, implementation, and evaluation process. The better the data, the better the plan, and the better and happier the student and teacher.

REFLECTION QUESTIONS

Q1. Thora is frequently out of her seat. The Language Arts teacher has come to you and expressed that Thora is *constantly* moving around the classroom and *never* gets work done. She is requesting that you develop a plan so that Thora will stay in her seat and complete work. What are your next steps?

Q2. You have a meeting scheduled with a family because they are concerned about their child's current grades, and several referral notices that have been sent home. You have been collecting frequency data on how often the child is either on task and off task during instructional times. How will you review those data with the family? What will your conversation sound like?

Q3. Go through the four-step problem-solving process using a current concern in your classroom. Be sure to include asking additional why questions to determine a root cause.

Q4. You collected baseline data for two weeks and have concluded that the behavior of concern occurs an average of twenty times per day. The team, the parents, and the student agreed to set a goal of less than five times per day within two weeks. After two weeks of the intervention the behavior is occurring fifteen times per day. What are questions the team could ask? What are possible next steps?

NOTE

1. Ohno, T., *Toyota Production System: Beyond Large-Scale Production* (Portland, OR: Productivity Press 1988), p. 17.

Chapter Eight

Who's in Charge?

CHANGING OUR OWN BEHAVIOR

Your health and happiness are the most important components to a long-lasting and fulfilling teaching career. Think of the last time you flew on a plane. You were likely reading a gossip magazine or getting in one more round on your candy game app while the flight attendant provided the in-flight instructions. One of the most poignant and important pieces of advice is given hundreds of times a day in midair: "In the event of a loss of cabin pressure an oxygen mask will drop from the ceiling. . . . *Be sure to adjust your own mask before helping others.*"

It is in our nature as humans—and especially as educators—to help all of those around us before ourselves. In the event of a loss of cabin pressure, there are only seconds available and you cannot help another if you are not safe first. The same concept applies to teaching. Place your health and happiness first and the health and happiness of your classroom will follow.

AVOIDING BURNOUT:
PATIENCE, THANKFULNESS, AND MINDFULNESS

The first hurdle to overcome is the idea that putting yourself first is selfish. Day in and day out we are selfless. Selflessness is one of many amazing traits that teachers seem to intrinsically possess. You have to practice being more conscious of yourself and your needs.

It is also true that teaching is often a thankless profession. It is often a job that is done day in and day out without nary a whisper of external gratitude. You may see the lightbulb go off for a student or see some measurable

75

successes, but that is not the same as personal thank-yous. Whether it is to be recognized publicly with loud cheers in a stadium or quietly as you pass a colleague, student, or parent in the hallway, it is natural to want to be recognized for the hard work that you do on a daily basis.

Affirmation and recognition are fuel for your spirit and perseverance. The words that you tell yourself are just as important as the words that you hear from others. In fact, being mindful of congratulating yourself can be even more powerful and lasting. Below are several tips to build thankfulness and gratitude toward yourself.

- Keep a gratitude journal: Document at least three things at the beginning or end of each day that you are thankful for. Focus at least one of those items on your teaching work.
- Be mindful and meditative: Set a timer on your phone's calendar or clock to gently remind yourself several times a day to stop and be thankful. Take a deep breath when you hear that chime; then orient yourself toward the great work you are doing in that moment or repeat a phrase of kindness (e.g., "I am grateful to myself for the work that I do. I am thankful for my persistence and resilience. I am honored to teach.").
- Flip your thoughts: If you find yourself letting negative thoughts in or blaming yourself for a lesson that didn't go well, a student that is being challenging, or a difficult conversation with a peer or colleague, take a deep breath, apologize to yourself for the negative thought, and replace that thought with a thank-you (e.g., "thank you for being strong enough to voice your opinion even though it challenged another's" or "thank you for taking the time to create an engaging lesson full of rich activities that will simply need to be shortened to be more effective").
- Count to three and ask, "Is it good for me?": In a fast-paced world quick responses are often expected. Instead of reacting automatically, take three seconds and ask if what you are thinking, what you are going to respond with, or what you intend to do is good for you. Taking that three seconds allows you the time to be reflective and self-aware.

MY PERSONAL BEHAVIOR PLAN

Another strategy is to understand that you are just as human and fallible as the students whom you work with. Many of the techniques that work to help with students' behavior will also work for yourself. Create a behavioral plan.

At the beginning of each new year, many people undergo the process of reinvigorating their diet or exercise regimen. If you begin a new diet plan, you start counting calories and reading ingredient lists. If you start running, yoga, or cycling, you track the days that you exercise and the length of time that you practice. These are data to help you make better decisions. These are your baseline data. These are the same data that you collect in the classroom to improve student behavior.

You can track the number of negative thoughts that you have in a day, the amount of time that you spend planning for meetings, or the number of e-mails that you respond to after work hours. With that information you can engage in the four-step problem-solving process that was described in chapter 7 and create a plan.

1. Identify the problem and the function.
2. Develop a plan.
3. Implement the plan.
4. Understand and evaluate the plan.

For example, imagine that you have been staying up late at least three nights a week responding to e-mails, grading papers, and working on a project for two of the committees that you support at school. Staying up late is affecting your personal and professional life because you are tired and not focused.

1. Identify the problem: You are staying up late to finish undone work. A probable function of the behavior is avoidance and attention (i.e., you are avoiding the consequences of colleagues and parents being upset that e-mails have not been responded to and work has not been completed. You also desire the attention for the work being done and being accepted and appreciated by your peers and administrators).
2. Develop a plan: You are going to commit one hour each day after work to responding to e-mails. You are going to delegate some of the work for the committee projects to colleagues. And you are going to send a letter home to families that a weekly e-mail update will be sent home on Fridays in lieu of responding to individual e-mails of a similar nature.
3. Implement the plan: Set timers and reminders each day to help stay focused on the plan. Create a simple newsletter template that can be easily updated and sent home weekly. Check in with colleagues on the project work.
4. Understand and evaluate the plan: Ask friends and coworkers if they see a difference in your energy and focus. Look at data on the number of hours spent working after work hours. Be reflective on aspects of the plan that may need to be tweaked. Make any adjustments and continue to implement and evaluate the plan.

Voila!

BEING THE BEST ME IN A GROUP OF WE

In the example above, committee work and responsibilities were mentioned. In the field of education there are often a number of additional duties that teachers perform on a daily or weekly basis. Many of those are committees or professional-learning community responsibilities. The work of these committees and groups is vital to the progress of the school and district. And, while it is vital, it is also time-consuming and requires a collaborative culture.

Collaboration is most often described as cooperating and/or working with another person or as part of a group. As a teacher, you likely orchestrate group work like a maestro in the classroom. You are able to identify groupings or pairings by learning style, reading level, or need. However, as adults, groups are often arbitrary and the work is likely not personalized based on interest or skill. So you may often feel stuck doing work that you are not passionate about. You may feel a lack of teamwork.

Two things most often occur in group work. Neither is collaborative in nature and neither will yield meaningful results. One is that no one takes responsibility for the work. Participants sit passively. No action plans are created. Little actionable work occurs. The other is that one or few people accept the burden of the work for the group. Actionable work occurs but it is not evenly distributed.

If you are participating in one of these group scenarios, make several simple shifts for the greater good.

1. Identify an aspect of the work that you enjoy, have passion for, or are skilled at. Focus your energy toward that piece or component of the work. If you are on a safety committee and you love riding bikes, focus your skills and strengths toward making the bicycle rider area safe and effective. You could organize a fundraising event for new helmets for the riders who cannot afford them. You could get volunteers to paint new lines in the parking lot for bike riders to follow. You could help build new safety racks for riders to park their bikes.
2. Actively participate. Others will see you engaged and may feel encouraged to be more active in the process. Be a role model. Ask questions. Listen intently. Take notes. Create plans. Encourage others to engage in the work. Allow positivity to be contagious.
3. Facilitate and delegate. Ask to become the leader of the group. Yes, it will require more time and commitment. However, you will also have more opportunity to make a difference. Use facilitative skills to allow the team to work collaboratively. Facilitation skills include:

   - guiding a group through a process
   - drawing upon the opinions and skills of others

- being a neutral participant
- creating a comforting environment
- developing structures and procedures
- supporting and cultivating ideas

Once the process is facilitative a structure for ensuring that work is distributed equitably can be introduced. Ask members to share out in round-robin formats during meetings. Have action plan templates that are used and reviewed on an ongoing basis. Utilize the team's strengths to determine roles in the group.

CHAPTER SUMMARY

This chapter focused on you. You are the most important piece of this puzzle. It is vital that you care for yourself so that you can be strong and healthy to care for others. Make plans and be a problem-solver to help in being productive and reflective. Focus your energy on being thankful, being a problem-solver, and being a true team member. Create plans, put plans into action, and evaluate their effectiveness on an ongoing basis. Stress and a lack of solutions to challenging classroom behaviors are most often cited as the reason for teacher burnout. Be the light that shines strong, not the light that burns out.

REFLECTION QUESTIONS

Q1. Make a list of the ways that you help to alleviate stress. How many of those items on your list are focused toward positivity? If some items are not, what are simple changes that you could make to refocus?

Q2. Use the four-step problem-solving process on a current issue/problem that you are having at school. What problem did you identify? What plan did you create? What plan did you put into place? How did the plan work?

Q3. Make a list of the committees or groups that you participate in. Does any of the work overlap? If so, could you assist in creating a more streamlined way of work? What would that committee/group look like?

Q4. What three things are you thankful for in this moment? Write them down.

Conclusion

Remember that you are the key to your happiness. You cannot rely on any other person or thing to bring you joy, hope, optimism, and happiness. The happiness that you carry with you can spread like moss on the sunny side of a tree. Each person can be touched by the happiness that you create.

A happy class is led by a happy teacher. A happy teacher uses the tools in his or her toolbox to build a successful foundation, strong walls, and a solid roof. That happy classroom will allow students the freedom and space to learn and grow into happy adults. That is ultimately the goal of educators.

While we conform to the demands of systemic teaching, testing, compliance, and committees, ultimately teachers love to teach and children love to learn. The key to cultivating and maintaining that love of learning is focusing on positive, strengths-based, individualized, and functional strategies.

As mentioned in the introduction, this book is intended for all teachers across all grade levels to build a toolbox of strategies, ideas, and interventions that will help in building a happy class. You are encouraged to try strategies for a period of time, collect data, determine effectiveness, and tweak strategies positively to make them work best for you in your classroom.

The chapters in this book have guided you from the foundation up. You have learned about organizing yourself and your classroom for success. You have learned about behavior and how to focus on the function of the behavior. You have been given strategies to address common classroom challenges. You have learned how to add positive strategies into the classroom. You have been guided through a problem-solving process and how to use data to help make decisions. And, most importantly, you have been brought back to the root of a happy class: you.

If you find yourself falling back into an old habit or routine, it's okay. It takes months to learn and integrate new behaviors. Don't give up. Refocus on the positive strategy and find small successes that help to motivate and encourage. Ask colleagues to provide feedback and recommendations. Rely on the strong community of partners that you have as an educator.

You can be the teacher of a happy class. You can even help others to create happy learning environments. You have the knowledge, skills, and willingness, and now you have a few more tools.

Go now, and grow your happy class.

Appendix
Additional Resources

Authentic Happiness: https://www.authentichappiness.sas.upenn.edu
Behavior Doctor Seminars: http://behaviordoctor.org
Center for Mental Health in Schools: http://smhp.psych.ucla.edu
International Institute for Restorative Practices: https://www.iirp.edu
Positive Behavioral Interventions and Supports: http://www.pbis.org
Positive Psychology Center: http://ppc.sas.upenn.edu
Vanderbilt University IRIS Modules Resource Locator: http://iris.peabody
.vanderbilt.edu/iris-resource-locator

Index

Antecedent, Behavior, and Consequence (ABC) data, 71
annual education plan, 69. *See also* individual education plan
antiseptic bounce, 42
attention signal(s), 14. *See also* transition prompt
attention, 22–23, 25, 26, 28, 30, 36, 48–49, 51, 60, 77
attention seeking, 22–23, 28, 48; non-contingent attention, 28; peer attention, 26, 28
avoidance, 21–24, 26–30, 36, 38, 43, 60, 77

baseline, 71, 77
behavioral plan, 66, 69, 76
behavior intervention plan, 66. *See also* behavioral plan
behavioral agreement, 11, 50, 66
behavioral momentum, 43

calming area, 7, 42, 47
chart game, 52
classroom management, 2, 4, 12, 30
classroom rules, 9–11, 19, 24, 49
collaboration, 6, 78

common planning, 2. *See also* planning
consequence, 10–12, 33, 36, 38; logical consequence, 12, 36

data-based decisions, 61, 65–66, 69
discipline, 10, 25, 34

equal choice, 48
escape, 22–24, 26–30, 36, 43, 47, 60
exclusion, 11, 24, 34–36, 38; exclusionary practices, 34–36, 38; non-exclusionary, 35–36; time out, 11, 24, 34–36; time out procedure, 34–35
expectations, 9, 49, 55, 61. *See also* school-wide expectations
extinction burst, 49

First-Then, 14, 46–47. *See also* Premack Principle; Grandma's Law; When-Then
functions of behavior, 11–12, 21–22, 26, 28, 30, 36, 49, 54, 62, 67, 77
functional behavior assessment, 71

Grandma's Law, 14, 47. *See also* Premack Principle; First-Then; When-Then

hierarchy, 11, 24, 44–45, 48;
consequence hierarchy, 24, 45, 48;
outcome hierarchy, 11, 44

impulsivity, 51
individual education plan, 66. *See also*
annual action plan
interest boosting, 46
intervention, 4, 11–12, 21, 27–28, 51,
54, 59, 63, 68, 71–72
intervention plan/strategies, 10, 27–28

learning modalities/styles, 5, 7, 13, 28,
45, 78

non-contingent attention, 28. *See also*
attention

observational recording, 71
office referrals, 11
operational definition, 68–69

partners, 2, 65, 68, 82; teaching partner,
2; Collaborating professionals, 65
peer attention, 26, 28. *See also* attention
planned ignoring, 48–49, 51
planning, 2, 4, 7, 13, 18, 23, 38, 46, 68,
77; Lesson plans, 2, 4, 7, 10, 13, 23,
68
positivity, 9–12, 28, 33, 49–50, 57–58,
61–62, 66, 68, 81–82
Positive Behavioral Interventions and
Supports (PBIS), 61–62
positive psychology, 61
praise, 28–29, 36, 43–45, 49–51, 61–62;
pivot praise, 49; positive praise, 28,
50, 62; specific praise, 44, 49; tangible
praise, 43, 45; verbal praise, 29
precise requests, 44
preferential seating, 47

Premack Principle, 14, 37. *See also*
Grandma's Law; First-Then; When-
Then
problem solving, 66, 68–69, 71, 77, 79
professional collaborator, 2–3
progress monitoring, 71
proximity, 71; proximity control, 71
punishment, 33–36, 38–39
punishment procedure, 35, 39

redirection, 42, 46
reframing, 58
reinforcement, 1, 9, 12, 14, 26, 28,
34–36, 43–45, 47, 49–53, 60, 62, 66;
rates of reinforcement, 43
rewards, 1, 9, 12, 14, 26, 36, 47, 49–53,
60, 62
replacement behavior, 25–27, 30, 62, 72
response to intervention, 66

scatterplot, 71–72
schedule of reinforcement, 28, 66
school-wide expectations, 9, 61, 67. *See
also* expectations
sensory, 7, 23, 25, 27, 30, 42
sensory input, 23, 25, 30
shaping, 51, 53
stimulus control, 14
successive approximations, 51–52

tangible, 23–24, 27, 30
token economy, 4, 35, 53–54, 62
transition prompt, 14

verbal de-escalation, 41–42

When-Then, 47. *See also* Premack
Principle; Grandma's Law; First-
Then
"withitness", 14